The Money Secret

Benjamin Holt

Work because you want to,
not because you have to

Disclaimer:

The following is presented for educational and/or entertainment
purposes only. Under no circumstances should it be mistaken for
professional investment advice, nor is it at all intended to be taken as
such. The commentary and other contents simply reflect the opinion of
the author alone on the current and future status of the markets and
various economies. It is subject to error and change without notice.

This book is dedicated to all those people that are strong enough to continue to educate themselves. There are too many people out there complaining how hard they work and how broke they are when there is a different way!

I also wish to dedicate this book to all my friends and family as without them lots of this book would not be possible. I have used them for many examples throughout this book as the stories are drawn from real life experiences that I have encountered.

Benjamin Holt

THE MONEY SECRET

FROM THE AUTHOR

"an investment in knowledge pays the best interest"
BENJAMIN FRANKLIN

The purpose of this book is to empower the minds of people with the initial education required about money. The fundamentals about money are not taught in school, we must learn it from somewhere and that somewhere is normally what your parents have taught you. Our habits are subconsciously imbedded in us from a young age. This book should open up your mind to make you think twice about your habits which include spending, saving and investing.

Irrespective of your age, your annual income or what profession you find yourself in, I believe there is something to be learnt for you out of this book so that you can have the desired lifestyle you have always wanted or dreamed of having.

With Australia being third behind India and China for how many millionaire's are created each day, and 95% of the worlds wealth occupied by a group of 5% of the population, there is no better time or reason to suggest that you cannot be the next millionaire!

Remember the worst thing you can do is do nothing. If you are standing still you are actually going backwards. What this means is that because of inflation, technology and advances in the world, if you are not at least doing something to keep up you are in fact falling behind and therefore going backwards. Your position relative to everything around you is getting worse.

By reading this book you are taking the step to action and just as education leads to knowledge, and working leads to a wage, this book can guide you to financial freedom and success!

Benjamin Holt

THE MONEY SECRET

CONTENTS

THE MONEY SECRET

CHAPTER 1
INTRODUCTION

Unfortunately in life we are all not privileged enough to be a princess Mary and run into our prince on a holiday in Sydney or be young and good looking enough to meet and marry a Hugh Hefner. Most of the population have to work hard 9-5 every day to make ends meet and survive. Surely, all the millionaires, multimillionaires and billionaires haven't slugged it out working 9-5 all the way up to the top by just earning a big wage. Surely, there must be ways to make money and be wealthy without having to work in the rat race our whole lives!

There are! This is a book to help you understand money, how to get it and what to do with it once you have got it. This will give you the opportunity to change the way you are currently living and make yourself a little wealthier and knowledgeable at the same time. There is no rule to say that you have to go to work every morning, every day, week in and week out. This is a choice that people make.

All the great speakers and educators like Tony Robbins, Robert Kiyosaki, Mal Emery, T Harv Eker, Napoleon Hill etc. all swear that nothing they say is new, and that everything they know has been learnt from someone else - they are just repeating it! I attended a Mal Emery workshop and he says "you don't get paid more to invent fire, someone has already invented it." Smart and rich people look for mentors and trails of success that they can mimic. Is there any point in making all the same mistakes that people have already made and trying to reinvent the wheel? You need successful mentors to learn from and follow. There is too much money involved for you to just put your money somewhere and just hope for the best.

My book incorporates what I have learnt from them. I am putting everything together that other people have taught me and putting it all into one place to help educate people so that you to, if you want it, can be rich as well. Ask yourself this question before you read any further; would you rather learn and take advice from someone that is flat broke or would you rather take advice from a millionaire? A perfect example of this is if you are employed by someone, doesn't matter who it is but simply you are an employee. You learn something different and want to implement it. Then the boss comes up to you and says, "Why are you doing that? Where did you learn that from?" If you say "I made it up and I think it will work." Do you think he will listen to you or just laugh you off? Because in his mind he thinks he is better than you. But if you say, "Oh, Henry Ford, or Greg Norman, or Donald Trump (whatever industry you're in) taught me this and said I should do it", then is your boss likely to have a different response than to just laugh you off? He might actually sit down and listen to you as the person that gave you this information is more successful than your boss.

A short story that I heard Robert Kiyosaki say and has repeated many times since is often replayed in my head. When he first met his wife Kim, (who by the way is about 10 years younger than Robert, she's a tall slim blonde girl) was flat broke but drove a brand new Mercedes. He said it doesn't matter if you don't have any money, you must act and look like you do!

2

People always have a perception of what they think of you, it doesn't matter if they say they don't, everyone is judgemental and they all have their own opinions. People judge others in many different ways such as where they live, what they dress like and what they drive. You need to have the perception that you are rich and successful.

I say this as from about the age of 10, I have been involved in property keenly watching my dad build and grow his portfolio. I say build as that's what he did, he built houses. This made his portfolio grow! During this time I acquired a lot of knowledge, I have done a lot of personal development courses, attended a number of schools, attained a university degree, a diploma, gained experience working with different property companies including commercial, worked in finance and of course being an entrepreneur with my father. For a period of time I never used my own money. Everything that I did was with my father and with my father's money. Irrespective of the knowledge that I had gained, because I technically didn't have anything in 'my' name no one would listen to anything I had to say. It wasn't until I turned 21 when I bought my first 2 investment properties and an XK Jag in 'my' name that people started to listen to what I had to say! From then on everyone thinks everything I have is designer and, whether it is my $30 pair of sunglasses or my $15 diamantes cufflinks everyone's perception of me has changed, they now think that I am rich, as I have the results. There is another saying that I like, 'don't tell me what you can do, show me your results!'

Robert tells that story about his car because he believes that when you are doing anything, you are not selling your product, you are selling yourself. People have to like and trust you, or they will not do business with you. Generally the first thing they ask you is "What do you have?" This book will teach you lots of things and help you get to where you want to be in life, because at the end of the day there is a deep underlying reason for why you want to be successful. You just need to work out what "it" is. Be it fame, fortune, helping others, a big house, fast cars, boats, planes or the opportunity to be free and do what you want when you want. However, without a burning desire to achieve and the willingness to do whatever it takes by putting in the work to learn and also implement what you learn, you just may not get to where you want to be.

I have often heard people say that knowledge is power; however, this is only partially correct. Knowledge is not power unless you apply the knowledge that you have gained.

THE MONEY SECRET

THE MONEY SECRET

CHAPTER 2
PEOPLE'S PERCEPTION AND
KNOWLEDGE OF MONEY

T Harv Eker teaches about your 'financial blueprint', or in other words uncovers your conscious thoughts and sub conscious thoughts about what you have already learnt about money. Who are the people that teach you about money? Generally your parents as they are the first port of call for everything you do in life from a very young age. You learn most things when you are little. In primary school they don't teach you about money, they merely teach mathematics, English, science, geography and a host of other things but not the fundamental strategies required to affect our money blueprint. The only time you have the chance to learn about money is when your parents talk about it. You hear and learn their perceptions when you are younger, it automatically becomes part of your thoughts and beliefs, it is entrenched in you through repetition and as you don't know any different you very rarely question it and accept it as truth.

As a result, whatever your parents think about money is what you also think about money. If your parents are shopaholics that go out and blow their money, most likely you are going to go out and do the same thing as that is what you have grown up with, seen and learnt. They are your mentors!

But what people have failed to understand is that your parents could have taught you the wrong thing about money, and that you have the ability to grow and change what you already know as well as your financial future.

If we use my parents as an example: My father is one who likes to spend his money. I'm sure you all would have heard the term, 'you spend money to make money', well this is what my father thinks and he has had no problem spending money. In fact, he loves it! This also meant that he had no respect for money and as a consequence he made some bad investment decisions and lost money on deals or as he would put it, he would lose money on "learning experiences". My mother on the other hand, is the opposite, she is a saver. She has a problem with spending $1. If she has to spend it she needs to have a good reason. Where did my mother learn this from? Well, from her Italian parents. I'm sure you may have heard Italian's are very tight with their money or as mum would put it, very careful with their money and they would not buy anything they couldn't afford to pay for. Mum hated debt, whereas dad would always say 'we need to leverage with other people's money. We need to buy investments that produce capital growth or provide us with an income.'

So over the years my dad has had to try and accommodate my mum's spending habits and try and make money. My dad was the entrepreneur that had a sense for money and how to make it, but also on occasions lose it, whilst my mother relied on her PAYG employment that provided a solid and reliable pay cheque every week whilst supporting dad and trying to bring some balance to the finances. Slowly but surely my mum has been working her way towards the middle and my dad has been working his way towards the middle so that they are now both smarter with their money and how they spend it. The way they have done this is through the jars system. This is where all of the income received gets allocated into the following categories. By just following this one simple system that I got from T Harv Eker, and even if you do nothing else from this book, you are destined to make a huge impact on your financial future!

1. **Financial Freedom Account (FFA)**
   This is a minimum of 10% contribution.
   This account is set up so that you can be in the position where you only work because you want to and not because you have to. This money should only be spent on investments that produce cash flow and/or capital growth.

2. **Long Term Savings For Spending Account (LSS)**
   This is a 10% contribution.
   The funds in this account go towards the things that you want, like a new car, new TV, a new holiday or anything else that you may want. This account has been great for my dad as he now understands that if he wants to buy something the money has to be in this account first. It has assisted in teaching him to respect money and not just spend it whenever he wants to.

3. **Education Account**
   This is a 10% contribution.
   The funds in this account go towards your ongoing education and personal development. For example: A seminar, university degree, an on line course or anything that enhances yourself as a person. In fact the money you used to purchase this book can come out of the education account.

4. **Charity Account**
   This is a 5% contribution
   Rich and prosperous people believe in giving back. If you give money away then more money will come back to you. There are people less fortunate than us out there and this is a little something from us that goes a long way for them. The giving starts immediately and is not reserved to when you are

wealthy for we need to learn how to give in order to be able to receive.

5. **Tax Account**

This can vary but as a general rule of thumb it is a 10% contribution.

Note: This account is only valid if you are self-employed and should be taken out first before dividing up into the other accounts. You do not need to set this account up if you are a PAYG employee as it will automatically be taken out before you receive your pay cheque.

6. **Play/Fun Account**

This is a 10% contribution.

As my mother is a saver and hates to spend money, this account has helped her to get used to the idea of spending money and to understand that it is ' ok.' The money in this account should be spent every month, or if you want to save up for something a bit more expensive, must be spent at least every 3 months.

7. **Necessity Account**

This is normally a 55% contribution.

This account is to pay for your essentials, electricity, gas, telephone, shelter, food etc. If you are living at home, you have lower expenses, less or no rent and you might not spend as much on food. If you have a balance left over this is when you can allocate the balance of the funds towards your financially free account or your long term savings for spending. This is why those accounts have a minimum of 10% contributions.

In school, children are not taught to strive or push themselves. These days the kids all get recognition for competing with participation medals and they don't keep score. I believe that this is wrong as in life, there are winners and there are losers. Equally as wrong is the expectation that to make money, you must follow the predictable path of going to school, getting an education, finding a job, buying a home and paying it off as quick as they can. This plan only works at keeping you in the rat race your whole life; it does not pave the way for you to become a millionaire.

Systems, such as the jars system, need to be in place as you need to be careful with what you do with your money. I say this system is very important and education about money is very important as I am sick of people complaining about how much they work and how broke they are. How many people do you know that started working when they are really young and always claim that they are broke? Yep, I know a lot of them as well! They spend their money on alcohol, cigarettes, drugs and going out, fast food chains and what they perceive to be 'having a good time.' This may be perceived to be a good thing, but surely we should allocate our money into the different categories so that we are always putting money towards being financially free, or as the younger people like to call it 'rich' so that they can enjoy having a good time for a lot longer and have more money to actually spend on these 'fun' things!

Quiz:

What did your parents teach you about money?

For example: "money doesn't grow on trees"

"what do you think I am made of money"

What else did they say?

Were they spenders or were they savers and what effect did this have on your growing up?

What did the school system teach you about money?

Do you want to get a good job so that you can buy a house and pay off your house as quickly as you can?

Do you know where and what you spend your money on?

Do you have a system in place for spending your money?

Need assistance to 'work because you want to and not because you have to?' Then get in touch with us and go to our website as we are here to help.

http://www.moneysecretsthatwork.com

THE MONEY SECRET

CHAPTER 3
WHY DO YOU WANT TO BE RICH?

Everyone has a different purpose in life and each individual wants to do different things with their money. For example, on 31st of December 2011, I met this lovely family heading into the city for the New Years Eve fireworks. I was talking to the 11 year old and I'm not sure how but we got onto the topic of money and he said that he wanted to be rich so that he could buy a Ferrari. So he has a goal, he knows what he wants and has a reason to want to be rich!

One of my best mates doesn't want to be rich; he likes working and has no desire to learn how to make money. He likes to work as it gives him something to do during the day. What he has failed to realise is that I have no problem with him working, that's why I call it, 'work because you want to, not because you have to.' If someone wants to work, let them! Being rich and having money just gives you more options in life.

I went to an Anthony Robbins seminar and he spoke about when people say to you that money isn't important, it means they are poor. The rich believe and know that money is important. He used the analogy of an arm and a leg to describe money and health, asking "what is more important?" We know they are both as important as each other. What if we had the best health in the world but you were homeless and living on the street and eating out of rubbish bins? Is this a very good quality of life? In my opinion not really, so that's why we need both in our lives, money and health!

He also said that people don't buy products they buy feelings. Like if you buy a Ferrari, you buy it because of what it makes you feel like. You may feel like superman, you may like the attention, either way you love what it does!

The example Tony used though was with women's hand bags. He asked the audience who has a nice hand bag? A lady put her hand up, he went over and asked her how much she paid for the handbag, to which she replied "I work there so I got it for a cheaper price."

Tony replied with "That's not what I asked, I said how much did you pay for the hand bag?"

She said $300. Tony then gasped, and so did the audience as this is a lot of money to spend on a hand bag. Tony then went on to ask the lady how much she thinks it costs to make the hand bag.

The lady and Tony came to a reasonable answer of $50. Tony then went on to his next example and asked the audience if anyone had a designer handbag such as a Gucci or a Chanel. A few ladies put their hands up and Tony went over to one and asked her "How much did you pay for the handbag?"

The response was "I got it on sale!"

"No, that's not what I asked you, was it?" says Tony as the whole audience laughs. So Tony is forced to ask the lady again how much she paid for it. This time she responds with "$1,000" and again the whole audience laughs as this is a lot more than the first lady. Tony then asks the lady how much she thinks it costs to make the handbag. Like the first lady it was significantly less than the price and they agreed that $100 would be a good enough answer.

Tony then asked the audience if anyone had a cheap handbag. A few ladies put their hand up and Tony went over to one of them and asked how much she paid for her handbag. The lady replied with $20. This response received a large amount of applause from the audience as it is a lot less than what the first two ladies paid. As with the first two ladies, Tony then asked how much she thinks it cost to make the handbag. She replied with $5 which everyone thought was a good enough answer.

The last thing that Tony did was ask all three women if they were happy with their purchases, which they all were. The moral of the story is that people don't buy products they buy feelings. Each lady spent significantly different amounts of money on their handbags and bought the same products made by different brands, yet they were all equally happy with their purchase. For each of them it tells a different story and shows that everyone wants to be rich for different reasons. Napoleon Hill says that "The starting point of all achievements is desire. Keep this constantly in your mind. Weak desire brings weak results, just as a small fire makes a small amount of heat." So you need to find your reason for desire and work towards that.

So now that we know that everyone has a different reason to be rich, we need to now redefine what the definition of rich means to you. Most of us define wealth as having LOTS of money and LOTS of things. How do you define when you are rich and decide that it is enough?

I was talking to this gentleman one time and he said that when he was a student, he dreamed of having his own car. So he worked very hard for 6 months and was finally able to buy a car. It was a 12 year old commodore, but he loved it and felt really cool! After a year and a half he bought a new car, but it did not feel as great, because there was an even cooler car at a dealership that he couldn't afford. No matter how much you have there will always be more! Being rich to you might mean having enough money to pay bills, putting some money away for when you need it and being able to give some money away to those who need it. Is it time you redefined your definition of wealth and what you want? What is your burning desire?

Quiz:

Do you want to be rich?

Do you know **why** you want to be rich?

Do you have a plan to get rich?

Do you know how much money you want to make in your life?

Do you know how much money you **need** to make in your life so that you can live the lifestyle you desire?

Need assistance to 'work because you want to and not because you have to?' Then get in touch with us and go to our website as we are here to help.

http://www.moneysecretsthatwork.com

THE MONEY SECRET

CHAPTER 4
WHY SOME PEOPLE NEVER GET RICH

Throughout this book I will expand on these points, but I want to give a quick summary first as to some reasons why people never get rich.

1. MOST PEOPLE WAIT TOO LONG TO START

You need to remember that property values go up and down all the time. Therefore, with this constant change in values, you are in property for the long term growth and not simply just to get in and get out straight away. The longer you wait to get started with your investing, the longer it will be before you get the money, success and freedom you want. It takes time for the power of compounding to work its magic.

Many people wait for everything to be perfect before they get going. Many investors are waiting for everything to be "perfect" before they get going. They wait for the right time in the cycle, the right property, the right economic environment or the right interest rates. Unfortunately, this often means they never get going as they are always waiting for something and always find an excuse not to do something. Why are they self-sabotaging?

2. FEAR STOPS THEM

Fear keeps many of us from getting what we want, that is why many men require alcohol to boost their confidence before talking to women. Money is the same. You work very hard for the money that you make so you find it difficult to invest it for fear that you might lose it.

I want you to be honest with yourself and think how many times has fear prevented you from taking action? It will probably be easier to relate this to a time when you have thought about trying to chat up someone you are attracted to, but have been too afraid because of the fear that they were too good looking and you would get rejected. Or you talk yourself out of saying anything because you think your pick up line won't work and they will think it's too cheesy. This fear might flow into your investing - you are afraid that you might get rejected, which is lose your money. Many people by not taking action and by being afraid have had many lost financial opportunities.

Whilst money is important and you work hard for it, no one ever likes losing money. Having said that, I have met a lot of rich people that have lost money and if you read about the successful people and listened to them speak, they have all lost lots of money at one point or another. On the other hand I have met lots of poor people that have not lost any money investing.

Whatever your fear is, for whatever reason you need to identify it so that you can move forward and take action. You would have heard the term in many movies for when alcoholics are in rehabilitation the counsellor says: 'The first step to recovery is admitting you have a problem.' Equally in finance, identifying your fears is the first step to moving forward to making you lots of money.

Successful investors have learned to harness their fears and rather than focus on the negatives, they use fear to force them into positive action. For example, rather than allowing the fear of debt to stop them taking on the commitment of buying a property they use the fear of not moving forward with their investments to motivate them. They use the fear of being stuck in their job for the rest of their lives, without the financial independence that they are craving, to motivate them to take on the commitment of an investment property.

Successful people have mentors and people that can help them and emulate from so that the fear is significantly reduced. I personally want more money to give me greater options in life, to provide for my family and to give my future partner the opportunity to do everything that she's ever wanted to do. I want to be successful for other people.

Just like a river, fear can be bridged. The river of fear is only as deep and as wide as you allow it to be. Once you've crossed that river of fear and experienced the success on the other side, you usually look back and wonder why you were ever afraid. But here's the catch: The only people who actually realise this are those that have crossed the river and who are now standing on the other side.

Money and success lives on the other side of fear.

3. WAITING UNTIL THEY KNOW ENOUGH/TOO HARD

This is a fear that I find is very strong but people don't want to admit it. They are happy to live in their own little bubble and just put everything into the too hard basket. This stops a lot of people from getting started. You will always have someone in your life that will tell you that it is too hard and give you a negative comment about it. This is not a reason not to learn something and shouldn't stop you from moving forward.

Once you start learning you will find lots of things that you don't yet know which then motivates you to keep learning. The way out is to recognise that while you don't know it all, and never will, you do know enough to get started with your investing and you will learn more along the way as you apply your knowledge in the real world, surviving any mistakes and challenges along the way. A perfect example of this is university. I did a four year property course at university and can attest that it is nothing like the real world. I did a Diploma of Finance and that too is nothing like the real world. Whilst you think you need to learn about everything, I want you to focus on property and investing your money into property as it appreciates in value over time and you don't need to learn everything as you can learn from the experiences of successful people.

4. Focusing on linear income instead of passive income

In my time I have found that very few people actually know what passive income or positive cash flow is. Because of this I have a whole chapter dedicated to explaining what it is. Firstly, you need to realise that not all income is the same, some are linear and some are passive. When I think about this topic I often think about something Robert Kiyosaki says:

"People often ask me how much my net worth is. I say I don't know, I would rather know how much my monthly passive income is."

Robert sets his goals for not net worth, but for passive income per month.

Linear income is what you get from a job. You work for an hour and get paid once for that hour's work, and that's it. Or in some cases, you might be on a salary and therefore don't get hourly pay, but either way, the bottom line remains the same; if you don't turn up to work you don't get paid.

Passive income is when you work once but continue to get paid over and over again for work you're no longer doing, so you are effectively making money in your sleep. The way to become wealthy is having passive income coming in whether you go to work or not. For example rent that comes in each week from an investment property, that is passive income.

That's what happens to property investors. Initially they work long hours, save up a deposit and then invest it into a property. Again, there are positive and negative properties but either way your property is appreciating in value. Rather than getting another job, the wealthy people know they need to send their money out to work for them rather than them go out and work for money themselves.

There is this one saying that my dad told me that is very important: "You work to learn not work to earn." I wrote this book to give you the opportunity to, 'work because you want to and not because you have to.'

If you're not making money while you sleep, you'll never become rich.

5. Not using systems for making money

Having a system in place for making money is something that takes the emotion out of your investment decisions and makes the results more reproducible. Emotions cloud a lot of people's judgements and it also makes you pass up many good investments because your emotions get involved. "Oh, I don't like that colour", or "I don't like the kitchen", or "it's only got 3 bedrooms". Don't make it personal, it's an investment property you're never going to live in it. Give the people what they want. I can't tell you how many times I have seen people pass up good investment opportunity because of their emotion or paid too much for an investment or a place to live out of emotion.

So in summary I will touch on this a lot more throughout the book but you need to have a system to make money, it's a formula. Much like the movie with Brad Pitt 'Moneyball' where they had a system for picking really good baseball players, this is the same with money. We have done many systems in property depending on the time of the market and what we believe is best to do. I will touch on some of these strategies later on in the book. But whatever strategy that you use, make sure you stick to it and if you have a proven system for making money, there is no limit to the amount of money that you can make.

6. NOT BEING PATIENT

Warren Buffest once said: **"wealth is the transfer of money from the impatient to the patient"**

To become a successful property investor requires patience and persistence. You must not only get started, but you must continue on and follow through. Residential property is a long-term investment. It's not a get rich quick scheme.

Yet many investors speculate rather than invest. They look for that "big deal" which will land them a jackpot in a short period of time. In general these types of deals rarely occur and, if you find one, they will usually be speculative in nature and more risky. I personally do the low risk deals and the ones that I know will make positive cash flow or capital growth. If I am making cash flow I don't care as much what the value's do. If I cannot get positive cash flow then I pick a low risk property that has shown good sustainable capital growth for a long period of time as then it is more likely to continue to provide me returns over a long period of time in the future. That's what property is, a long term strategy.

You don't have to look for the latest fads or the latest speculative growth areas but if you want to speed things up a bit you can help create your own capital growth through buying a good property at a fair price, then adding value through refurbishments, renovations or redevelopments. By doing this you are manufacturing your own capital growth.

Decide to do these six things that successful property investors do and you are much more likely to become a successful and wealthy property investor. If you don't do them, then like most people, you may never get rich.

Quiz:

What is your fear?

Why haven't you invested?

Is your fear or reason for not investing under one of the above six headings?

If you have invested already, were you ever afraid?

Do you have anything generating passive income? I.e.: do you have anything making you money while you sleep?

Need assistance to 'work because you want to and not because you have to?' Then get in touch with us and go to our website as we are here to help.

http://www.moneysecretsthatwork.com

CHAPTER 5
NOTHING HAPPENS BY ACCIDENT

Have you ever made any money by accident? Maybe you were walking down the street one day and found a 2 dollar coin lying there or someone has dropped a 5 cent piece and couldn't be bothered picking it up. Or how many times have you seen a 2 dollar coin on the ground, and when you bent down to pick it up, someone has played a trick on you and it was in fact stuck to the ground!

Whilst this does happen sometimes, no one just hands you money! You need to work for money and there is a formula to make it. Lots of people have made money in the past and have already made all the mistakes. Is there any point in trying to reinvent the wheel when you can just follow other people and what they have done to become successful?

One of the common things that all successful people have is that they write their goals down, they all have something to achieve. I remember attending a speech by Margaret Court who is the best ever female tennis player in the history of the game and no one man or female has won more titles than her. She told her story about her career and when she was playing, what she gave up and the things that she wanted to achieve in her life. At each point of her life, she had a certain goal that she was working towards. Once she reached it, she made a new one. This drove her desire to be the best and to continue playing. It's no coincidence that she ended her career a second time as she had achieved everything that she wanted to achieve in tennis.

Goals and dreams are important, otherwise you are not

working towards anything and you just live day by day. Even when you are taught the typical thing about money (go to school, get a job, buy a house and pay it off as quickly as you can) this is still a plan that you are working towards. What happens when you pay off your house? Then what? You always need to continually update your goals and plans.

Have you thought what would happen if you decided to build a house with no plans? If you want to make something you need a recipe or a plan otherwise you are going to end up with a mess. This is something that is no different in making money. To become financially free it doesn't just happen, you actually need to work for it and come up with a way for legally acquiring money, as you don't just make money by accident.

It doesn't matter how short or long your goals list is - there is no right or wrong answer. Napoleon Hill says that your goals should be precise and have a time limit on them. For example by the 1st of January 2015 I would have accumulated $100,000 in my bank account.

You also need to set personal goals that are not just about money. I remember my dad telling me that you can't just set all your goals about money "all work and no play makes Benjamin grumpy. All play and no work makes Benjamin broke." You need to have a balance. How you make and set your goals is completely up to you but just make sure you do it as that is your plan, your recipe, and without it you will just go around in circles. You must have balance in your life.

GOALS

You might be confused about what kind of areas that you might like to write goals for. I have categorised some goals into different groups for you:

Health

Family

Community

Social

Education

Spiritual

Business

Financial

These are just examples of some of the areas that create balance in your life. I personally have goals that are for the Month Ahead, the Year Ahead and also the Long Term.

You can make your goals list as long or as short as you want.

I encourage you to pick up a pen and a piece of paper and jot down the goals you want to reach. Look at each goal and **evaluate** it. Make any changes necessary to ensure it meets the criteria for a **SMART goal**:

S = Specific
M = Measurable
A = Attainable
R = Realistic
T = Timely

Specific

Goals should be straightforward and emphasize what you want to happen. Specifics will help you focus your efforts and clearly define what you are going to do.

Specific is the What, Why, and How of the SMART model.

WHAT are you going to do? Use action words such as direct, organize, coordinate, lead, develop, plan, build etc.

WHY is this important for you to do it at this time? What do you want to ultimately accomplish?

HOW are you going to do it?

Ensure the goals you set are very specific, clear and easy. Instead of setting a goal to lose weight or be healthier, set a specific goal to lose 2cm off your waistline by 23 March 2014 or to walk 5kms each day before 9am at a challenging pace.

Measurable

If you can't measure it, you can't manage it. In the broadest sense, the whole goal statement is a measure for the project; if the goal is accomplished, there is a success. However, there are usually several short-term or small measurements that can be built into the bigger goal.

Choose a goal with measurable progress, so you can see the change occur. What will you see when you reach your goal? Be specific! "I want to read 100 pages of 'Think and Grow Rich by Napoleon Hill before the 25th of October 2013" shows the specific target to be measured. "I want to read a lot" is not as measurable.

Establish concrete criteria for measuring progress toward the attainment of each goal you set. When you measure your progress, you stay on track, you reach your target dates, and you experience the exhilaration of achievement. This spurs you on to continued effort to reach your other goals.

Attainable

When you identify goals that are most important to you, you begin to figure out ways you can make them come true. You develop the attitudes, abilities, skills, and financial capacity to reach them. You begin seeing previously overlooked opportunities to bring yourself closer to the achievement of your goals.

Goals you set which are too far out of your reach, you probably won't commit to doing. Although you may start with the best of intentions, the knowledge that it's too much for you means your subconscious will keep reminding you of this fact and will stop you from ever giving it your best.

A goal needs to stretch you slightly so you feel you can do it and it will need a real commitment from you. For instance, if you aim to lose 10kgs in one week, we all know that isn't healthy or achievable. But setting a goal to lose .5kg and when you've achieved that, aiming to lose a further 0.5kg will keep it achievable for you.

The feeling of success which this brings helps you to remain focused and motivated.

Realistic

This is not a synonym for "easy". Realistic, in this case, means **"do-able."** It means that the learning curve is not a vertical slope; that the skills needed to do the work are available; that the project fits with the overall strategy and goals of the organization. A realistic project may push the skills and knowledge of the people working on it but it shouldn't break them.

Devise a plan or a way of getting there which makes the goal realistic. The goal needs to be realistic for you and where you are at the moment. A goal of never again eating sweets, cakes, crisps and chocolate may not be realistic for someone who really enjoys these foods.

For instance, it may be more realistic to set a goal of replacing a daily chocolate bar with a piece of fresh fruit. You can then choose to work towards reducing the amount of sweet products gradually as and when this feels realistic for you.

Be sure to set goals that you can attain with some effort! Too difficult sets the stage for failure, but too low sends the message that you aren't very capable. Set the bar high enough for a satisfying achievement!

Timely

Set a timeframe for the goal: e.g. I would have researched two investment properties by Wednesday 30 June 2013. Putting an end point on your goal gives you a clear target to work towards.

If you don't set a time and the commitment is too vague, it tends not to happen because you feel you can start at any time. Without a time limit, there's no urgency to start taking action.

Time must be measurable, attainable and realistic.

Everyone will benefit from goals and objectives if they are SMART. SMART, is the instrument to apply in setting your goals and objectives.

Quiz:

Do you have a formula in place for making money?

Do you have any goals?

Do you read them?

Do you know what they are?

Do you carry them with you?

Need assistance to 'work because you want to and not because you have to?' Then get in touch with us and go to our website as we are here to help.

http://www.moneysecretsthatwork.com

CHAPTER 6
COMPOUNDING
INTEREST/OPPORTUNITY COSTS

There will always be success! History has shown all the difficulties and obstacles that have had to be surmounted and yet despite of them there has still always been success.

Living in Australia we are all so privileged. Australia is third behind India and China for how many millionaires are created per day. If we are in such a powerful position and there is always success. I ask the question, "Why can't it be you?"

Let's take a personal example. If you got home and your partner said to you "you're not important to me" how do you think you would feel? I personally know I would feel pretty horrible. I don't think your partner would feel very attracted to you if you said that to them. So why is money any different?

One of my pet peeves in the world is people not understanding and respecting money. For you to be successful in life, be rich and financially free you need to respect money! This is something that I don't think people quite get the grasp of.

Another thing that people don't understand is that you can get rich off the money that you are wasting! It doesn't matter how much money you make, what matters is how you spend your money and how much of it you keep. When the famous Michael Jackson died he had 500 million dollars worth of debt! This even after all the money that he has earnt! To this day it is still not all paid off. I'm sure everyone has also heard of the famous boxer Mike Tyson, the one that bit off another guy's ear. Well he had a net worth of $400 million, yet he went broke as well. Even if you put you're 400 million in the bank earning 3% interest that's 12 million a year. How hard is it to live off 12 million a year? In Mike Tyson's case, very hard! Just as millionaires can lose and waste money, so can you - it is very easy to do. Would you be as wasteful if you had 4 million dollars or would you have a plan in place to have the money work for you?

Compounding interest and opportunity costs are very important to me as I have played a lot of sport and heard a lot of stories about people just throwing away their money. They are missing out on the value that this money that they are throwing away can bring and the riches that it can produce. The most common phrase I hear is "oh it's only 2 dollars more expensive" or "oh, it's only 200 dollars that I blew last night at the pub, it doesn't matter". Well if this happens every week it adds up to a lot of money over time! People are ignorant of the fact that they are not respecting the money that they have. Having money is a privilege. It should be respected and not just thrown away. It is a very powerful tool if used correctly.

The first thing that you need to do is value every dollar that you make. There is no point throwing it away because how many of you actually like your work and working in the workforce? How many of you complain on a Sunday that you have to go to work on a Monday? You all work hard for your money, yet at times it gets thrown away so easily! Although you might think a dollar doesn't get you very far, it's not even half a Mars bar and you don't care if you use it or you lose it.

You see, prosperous people do not think this way about a dollar coin, they see it as a money seed that has the power to grow into something bigger and better. Trees don't start off massive just like adults don't come out of the womb fully grown, they start out small and they grow over time. This is the same as a dollar coin, it will grow and become a massive tree!

So if a dollar a day is so small to you and you don't care if you spend it or if you lose it, then can you afford to put away a dollar a day? In a few short years, your money tree will be fully grown and majestic, growing right in the centre of your future dream home. Imagine that! Branches of your money tree spreading along the ceiling into every room of the house. Every few meters or so is a nodule which pops open once or twice a day—and releases the fruit of the tree—a crisp one hundred dollar note. That hundred gently floats down and lands in the strategically placed basket. All night long you hear the pop, pop, pop as these nodules open and release their fruit, your money tree is producing fruit, whilst you sleep, whilst you work, whilst you play and whilst you eat. It never stops; it's an endless stream of cash flow, 24 hours a day, 7 days a week and 365 day a year.

That's why it is so important to preserve and protect each of these money seeds which is simply just a dollar a day. Every time you waste one of those silly little coins it's just like throwing away a money seed. No seed, No tree. This tree is a bit like a baby, at the start you need to spend a lot of time with it to make sure that it grows up ok, but then when it gets to a certain age it can now look after itself; this is the same with money. If you put a dollar coin in a bank account at 3%

it would take 468 years to become a million dollars. So every time you earn a dollar you put it into this bank account it starts to compound.

So at the start as it's a baby, let's say you put away $200 per month. If you're living at home that should be very easy. So instead of 3% you are a little bit better and can invest it at 20% a year which is only 1.66% per month. A simple naked put option produces you 4-8% per month. Or what if you leveraged your money? So $200 per month at 20% for 20 years grows into $632,000. Now instead of starting today you um and ah about what to do, is it good or not? So this will leave you with only 19 years of growth instead of 20, how much is in your bank account 20 years from today? It's only $516,000. That's $116,000 less than what you could have had if you had started on schedule. Did everyone remember one of the reasons people don't become rich, they wait too long before they start. In other words, your procrastination cost you $116,000 future dollars! Procrastination is expensive.

For each of the 365 days that you waited, your future portfolio was shrinking by over 300 dollars.

(116,000 / 365= $317.81) In other words, every day you put this plan off, costs you $300 future dollars per day. Every hour you wait costs you more than $13. You are wasting 13 dollars an hour, 24 hours a day. So for all of you out there who would of started work in your early teenage years you could have been doing this for years now and got a massive head start on the early development of your tree and before you know it you could just have your money sitting there earning you interest.

I am not saying if you do everything in this book that you will become rich straight away this is not a get rich quick scheme. Money takes effort and you need a plan and work towards that plan to achieve your goals. There may be failures along the way but we learn from our mistakes. Napoleon Hill has many powerful messages and quotes in his book 'Think and Grow Rich' and has sold approximately 70 million copies; he says "Before success comes in any man's life, he is sure to meet with much temporary defeat, and, perhaps, some failure. When defeat overtakes a man, the easiest and most logical thing to do is to quit. That is exactly what the majority of men do. More than five hundred of the most successful men this country has ever known told the author their greatest success came just one step beyond the point at which defeat had overtaken them." The moral to this story is to never, never, never give up. In 1969 man walked on the moon, but it is a well known fact that Apollo 11 which took them there was in fact only on course 3% of the time. The rest of the time it was adjusting and correcting its course so that it could finally reach its target. You should look at life the same way, always correcting and adjusting to achieve your goals and target.

Quiz:

Do you respect money?

Do you throw away a dollar and don't think twice about it?

Do you like going to work on a Monday morning?

Have you starting making your own money tree?

Need assistance to 'work because you want to and not because you have to?' Then get in touch with us and go to our website as we are here to help.

http://www.moneysecretsthatwork.com

CHAPTER 7
HOW MUCH MONEY DO YOU EARN?

I want to start off this chapter by asking you a few questions to get you thinking big and thinking about what you actually want!

What are you currently earning?

What would you like to earn?

1. How much money do you need on a weekly basis to 'do all' the things you truly love?

2. In how many years from now do you want 'it all'?

For most people you are employed by someone and you are on a yearly wage or you get paid by the hour. Either way your salary is limited, however, you may receive a one off Christmas bonus each year if you're lucky! There are only 24 hours in a day and 7 days in a week. How many of those hours do you actually want to spend working let alone commuting backwards and forwards to work? The point that I am trying to make here is that there is a limit to the amount of money that you can make because there are a finite number of hours in a week.

There can be lots of money to be made by being an employee and lots of benefits as well, for example sick leave, you still get paid while you are sick. If you own your own business or are self-employed you don't get paid if you are sick. You also have a lot less stress as it is not your company so therefore you are not as invested in the company and your priorities are not the same as the owner of the company.

What if you were smart with your money and invested it wisely so that you would be able to increase your income and maybe be able to work less and work because you want to and not because you have to?

Do you want to go through life as a high income earner who under-invested in assets that appreciated in value over time?

There is nothing wrong with people earning high amounts of money per year, but you need to be smart with it. A lot of people would rather go on a holiday and sit out in the sun and get a tan than invest that money into property. If you are smart with your money you will use the Jars system, or bank accounts set up which are designed so that you can have both the life style and quality of life that you choose.

For those of you who have already forgotten the Jars system here it is again!

1. FFA (Financially Free Account) which is a minimum of 10% of your income
2. LSS (Long Term Savings for Spending) also 10% of your income
3. Fun - again 10% of your income and to be spent every month
4. Education - 10% of your income and for your education to continue to learn and emulate rich and successful people
5. Tax – only for those who are self employed, as the PAYG has tax taken out prior to being paid, 10% of income prior to distributing to all of the other accounts.

6. Charity – 5% of income
7. Necessity – this is initially set at 55% but can vary at the start and in some cases until you get yourself under control it may be as high as 110% of your income as you spend more than you earn and put it on credit card.

Another issue with high income earners is that you pay a larger amount of tax; you may lose half your income to the tax man! As this happens you end up being around the normal wage again but yet you have a more expensive life style, you drive nice cars, live in a nice suburb and send your children to private schools. The more you earn the more you spend and at the end of the day you still live from pay cheque to pay cheque. If something were to go wrong and you could not work, everything would come falling down like a stack of cards. People must learn to live within their means and spend less than they earn. This does not necessarily mean going without, it means spending wiser and of course sometimes having to wait a little longer to get what you want; this is called delayed gratification.

I would like to tell you a story about a friend of mine who is a low income earner. I was living in England playing cricket for 6 months and I went with my mate Fred, (that's not his real) to Windsor Castle for the day. On the way there we stopped off at the ATM as he had no cash and wanted to get some. He took out 110 pound and I said "Wow, that's a lot what are you using that for?"

He replied with "The weekend."

I said, "The weekend, what are you going to spend 110 pound

on over the weekend?"

"Booze" he said.

Now you can imagine how shocked I was as I do not drink for many reasons but one of them is how much money you can blow on alcohol. Now to me this was a large amount of money to simply drink away in 2 nights. My mind immediately thinks how much money that is per year and what I can invest with that money and how much money I can make with it. His mind thinks how he won't remember the night before and how much of a good time he will have without remembering it. So we have contrary beliefs.

On the way back from a cricket game that I was playing the following day I was telling this story to my host in the car, saying that I couldn't believe how much money he was just drinking away, literally. To my surprise, my host said "I would love to only spend 110 pound on booze in a weekend." What shocked me most about this is that my host couple kept telling me they couldn't afford stuff and telling me off for leaving my windows open as they couldn't afford it if something were to happen. Now you can only imagine how shocked I was when I heard him say that he would love to "only spend 110 pounds on booze"! I cannot believe how people cannot see the value of money and how powerful it is and how much they are seriously drinking away in comparison to their income before they even start paying for their essentials.

So I thought to myself, maybe these guys are not actually seeing how much money they are throwing away before they start spending money on important things.

If you're a low income earner and you complain that you can't afford things, think to yourself how much of your income are you throwing away? Instead of saying you can't afford something, change your mind set by changing the words you use and ask yourself a different question. The new question you should ask yourself is: **"How can I afford it?"** Whether it's a new car, a holiday, a weekend away, new clothes, a new house etc. etc.

If you are earning $50,000 a year, you take out tax and superannuation and you are now down to $41,703 a year that you are earning. Now, this is a lot less than what you actually thought!

Then, you might smoke 1 packet a day; let's say the average is $24 per pack that's $8,760 per year, so you're now down to do $32,943 per year. Again this is a lot less than the $50,000 per year that you thought you were earning.

Then you have a few drinks, spending $100 a week (and I am being generous for some of you!) So that's another $5,200 per year (conservative figure). That leaves you with $27,743 per year to spend on everything else before paying for any essentials let alone spending money and having money for investing and holidays. But yet I'm sure if you ask them why they can't do something they will say because they can't afford it. Now compare that $100 per week to the story I told about my friends. 110 pound per week in today's currency (when I was writing the book) is $170 which is $8,866, leaving your income at $24,077. I would hate to think he would be doing that when it was $3 to the pound!

One of the reasons people don't change where they are in life is because they are happy with where they are now. If you really aren't happy with being fat, or unfit, or not having enough money, or the relationship you are in, then you should actually make it a priority and do something about it to bring change so that you are happy! What part of your life are you not happy with at the moment? What do you need to change? What do you need to prioritise? I would suggest now would be a good time to grab a pen and a piece of paper and write them down, prioritise them and do something about them (when I say a pen and piece of paper that is what I actually mean so that you can carry it with you and focus on them not just type them into a computer and forget all about it and never look at them again).

Quiz:

Do you live on one pay cheque at a time?

Are you a high income earner that has under invested in assets?

Do you know where your money is being spent?

Need assistance to 'work because you want to and not because you have to?' Then get in touch with us and go to our website as we are here to help.

http://www.moneysecretsthatwork.com

THE MONEY SECRET

CHAPTER 8
POSITIVE AND NEGATIVE CASH FLOW

A lot of people don't understand what this is and think that investment properties are negative cash flow, or also known as negatively geared. On the other hand there are also properties that are positively cash flowed also known as positively geared.

Most properties in Australia are what are called 'Negatively geared' properties. This is when the income you receive from the property (which is the rent), is not enough to cover all the expenses. These expenses are generally the interest repayments to the bank and also the agents' commissions, fees, body corporate fees, rates, taxes etc. 'Positively geared' properties on the other hand are when the income you receive from the property is higher than all your expenses. So after you pay all your expenses that property pays you money every week i.e.: putting money into your pocket.

People say to me all the time that they want to purchase negatively geared properties for tax purposes. This is fine but wouldn't you rather make more money? Or purchase property that you get a negatively geared benefit but with the positive cash flow?

To people that tell me this I ask them how much tax would you rather pay?

- $0
- $1,000
- $1 million
- or $10 million.

Now I would like you to ask yourself this exact same question. How much tax would you rather pay?

Most people answer $0. But think; how much income do you have to earn per year to pay $0 in tax? The maximum is around $15,000 per year (give or take as it fluctuates depending on the government). Do you really want to earn $15,000 per year? Think of the amount of money per year that you have to make to pay 10 million dollars a year in tax! That's the kind of money I know I want to be making! So in essence if you pay more tax, you make more money. I don't understand why people have a problem with making money? Yes, there are ways we can reduce tax but it's the principle and concept of the fact we need to make the money first to reduce the amount of tax we pay.

Most properties in Australia are negatively cash flowed because of the high interest rates and the low yields (rent vs. the property value). As property values in Australia are so high, people cannot afford to pay high rents for the properties. People also think the more expensive areas are the areas that have the highest rental yields. This is in fact not true. The most expensive suburbs have the lowest rental yields as the property values are so high even with the higher rent it doesn't compare to the price. So as the price is so high the mortgage repayments are significantly higher than the rent that you will receive from the property. In a lot of cases the only way to reduce the repayments is by putting a lot more of your cash into the property. But you could effectively buy a whole other property with that money that you had.

You should be aware that there are positive and negative cash flow properties; and the area that you buy in can affect your rental yield. This in turn can affect the amount which a property is positively or negatively cash flowed.

There are still benefits to purchasing negatively cash flowed properties in expensive areas provided these areas have proven long term historical capital growth (which could be one of your strategies). You could also buy in the new up and coming suburbs that have a high socio economic status i.e.: the income per household in that area is high. One of the issues with this strategy of course is each time you obtain a negative cash flow property you are reducing your borrowing capacity; you then have to find a way to earn more money in order to service your new debt. The other issue you can have is during a period of negative capital growth, higher interest rates, stricter borrowing guidelines from lending institutions; any negatively cash flowed strategy must be supported by either a positive cash flow property strategy or a secondary means of increasing your income and cash flow not related to you working for money on an hourly basis.

CHAPTER 9
CASH FLOW VS. CAPITAL GROWTH

One of the most important wealth creation principle's you must know is that it is your net worth that increases over time due to the capital appreciation in your property. It is capital growth and not income that makes you wealthy, whereas cash flow gives you quality of life and lifestyle. I suppose another way to put it is that being wealthy is the destination, whereas the cash flow along the way is the journey.

Property remains the single biggest source of wealth with 49 real estate entrepreneurs in the BRW richest 200 list, and many of those who didn't make their wealth in property, store their wealth by investing in property.

If you study the average growth of property in Brisbane, Sydney and Melbourne since 1967 you will discover that these markets have enjoyed more than 2000% growth in this time! In the more recent years we have even seen one of the worst financial crisis in our lifetimes and yet the Australian property market has continued to hold strong and the average long term growth rate of all property in Australia is 9% per annum which is a property doubling in value every 8 years. Of course, we all know that some property does grow at a higher rate than this and some at a slower rate. Therefore, in order to assist you to determine whether or not to invest in a particular area we can look at how long a particular property will take to double in value based on its long term historical capital growth. Are we likely to continue the high property growth that we have seen in the past or is the property cycle now slowing and likely to remain that way for some time? What is the right investment strategy for you to move forward? Should you purchase property for cash flow or for capital gain?

Recently Gail Kelly, CEO of Westpac, warned that Australia is unlikely to ever again see the type of housing boom that sparked a massive rise in personal wealth in the past decade.

At around the same time Reserve Bank of Australia governor Glenn Stevens said the RBA was not trying to "engineer a return to a housing price boom" by lowering interest rates.

To determine which is more important, let's look at what each strategy provides.

Positive Cash flow

In brief, positive cash flow property means that you will not be out of pocket each week after receiving the rent, paying the loan interest and other expenses, and claiming the appropriate depreciation. Each week you are getting paid to own a property which in 10 years time is going to be worth more money that what you paid for it today.

While positive cash flow properties are sometimes hard to find, they are there and we have access to them! If positive cash flow properties are putting money in your pocket every week then there are fewer limitations as to how many properties you can actually purchase. Investors are limited by their ability to repay the mortgage repayments based on their income. So for each positive cash flow property you purchase your income and therefore, borrowing capacity is increased.

Capital Gain

The problem for an investor seeking high capital growth property is that property prices in the desired areas often increase faster than the rental returns; meaning week in and week out you are paying money out of your income to own this property. For many families, unless you have a high income, this could be a problem. Unlike the positive cash flow where your income is increased by each property you purchase, for each property you purchase with high capital gain or negative cash flow, it decreases your income therefore reducing your borrowing capacity, limiting the amount of properties you can actually purchase.

So how do you know which one to choose?

The answer will depend on your own personal goals and circumstances. When you buy a property you should be looking at how to find a profitable deal. It is not about finding any property - you buy property for the numbers and not for the emotion. What is the point in buying something if you are not going to get some sort of benefit out of it? But why should you invest at all? Well 92% of Australia will retire at 65 on less than $15,000. If this is the kind of lifestyle you want to live when you are older and you think you can rely on the pension or your "industry super" and you have no investment strategy, well then keep doing what you are doing now. If this is not where you want to be, then now is the time to take action and make some changes and do something different to find a way to make yourself more money so that you can work because you want to and not because you have to.

Whether you prefer the high rental yield from positive cash flow property or high capital growth from your investment property, or a combination of both, the success of your investment will depend on your total returns – rental income and capital growth. It also depends if you are prepared to go to bed every night and hope that your property goes up in value before you are making any money or if you are happy to make money whilst you are sleeping week in and week out whilst still owning bricks and mortar.

If sitting, waiting and praying for your property to go up in value doesn't sound like the best investment strategy for you, then sign up to our website and mentoring program and we can show you how to get the lifestyle and quality of life that you always wanted!

Where are you in life?

One of the most important aspects to purchasing an investment property is to establish your reasons for purchasing and where you are in life to get the most benefit out of investment properties.

When you are starting out growing your property portfolio i.e.: are younger, you need to leverage your money as much as you can and borrow as much money as you can. It's not quite the same when you're a little bit older as you may want to have less debt and therefore put more cash into it. The more cash you put into the investment means the returns you get will be higher as you have less repayments meaning you have more cash flow. As you have more money invested into the deal you are missing out on a little bit of wealth creation through opportunity costs.

A perfect example of leverage and opportunity costs is if you have $40,000 and you want to invest it. When you're younger and trying to grow your portfolio you should try to split that amount in half and purchase two investment properties. You could purchase one for capital growth and one for cash flow to offset the other property. Whereas when you're older you should consider only buying one for cash flow rather than capital growth as there is less point trying to invest for the long term as you need to enjoy life now. So that means with the same amount of money that you have, you have now double the leverage on your money and bought two properties going up in value instead of one. So you will be earning twice the amount of wealth as what you would with one, but since you have used more borrowed funds your cash flow for the two properties will be less.

Purchasing positively cash flowed properties means that you are receiving money right here and right now. Each week you are getting paid to own your property, it is another source of income.

Remember, capital growth gives you wealth whereas cash flow gives you life style. Depending on what you need out of life, and where you are in your life will determine which one is more important to you. I personally believe the best thing is to get both.

To highlight the difference, let's have a look at the same property but one with a National Rental Affordability Scheme (NRAS) benefit which will make the property positive cash flow and the other a standard investment property.

NRAS – a new asset class?

Before we go any further I need to explain what the National Rental Affordability Scheme (NRAS) is. Australia is suffering from a chronic housing shortage, with the National Housing Supply Council estimating in a recent report that there is a shortfall of 254,800 dwellings across the nation. This gap is predicted to increase to over 640,000 in the next 20 years. This shortage of houses means that rental vacancies are at an all time low which in turn is now causing rents to rise and making it very difficult for low to middle income earners to firstly afford and secondly even find decent affordable rental properties.

In order to combat this developing crisis, the Federal Government has made hundreds of millions of dollars in grants available to residential property investors in an effort to help supply and keep pace with the skyrocketing demand for housing.

While NRAS is highly beneficial to tenants, the returns available to investors through this scheme are unlike any other property investment opportunities currently on the market.

In exchange for landlords offering tenants a modest 20-25% discount on the market rent, e.g. a property normally rented out at $300 per week would rent under NRAS for $225 to $240 per week and the Government would provide the investor with a tax free payment each year for a 10 year period. The payment for this year is $9,981, or equivalent to $191 per week which also increases over time as it is indexed to inflation.

This means that for many investors their NRAS property will actually be cash flow positive after all expenses. While most investment properties initially cost their owners money on an ongoing basis, positive cash flow NRAS properties provide investors with an income, it puts money in your pocket rather than taking money out of your pocket. Remember cash flow gives you life style whereas capital growth gives you wealth. It is this passive income that will eventually allow you to work because you want to not because you have to.

Here is a typical example of an NRAS property at work versus and non NRAS property. They are two identical properties in the same street next door to each other.

POSITIVE V NEGATIVE		
PROPERTY: $375,000. 100% financed ($388,700 inc expenses); 6.25% interest-only loan, 30 year term; 32.5% Marginal Tax Rate; NRAS rental discount 30%		
	NRAS	**NON-NRAS**
Rental	$13,650	$19,500
Total Expenses	$44,658	$44,048
LOSS	$31,008	$24,548
Tax Reduction	$10,244	$8,346
Depreciation	$12,100	$12,100
Base net cash flow	-$8,664	-$4,102
NRAS incentives	$9,981	
Net Cash Flow	$1,317	-$4,102
Net Weekly Cash Flow	$25	-$79

Note: the example above demonstrates a rent discount of 30% when my model of choice Ethan Affordable Housing has a 20% discount. For more information on Ethan Affordable Housing and the properties that they have available check them out via my web site.

http://www.moneysecretsthatwork.com

The difference in cash flow per year, that is money that goes into your pocket, and remember in most cases it is tax free, and these two properties are identical, is $5,408 per year or over $54,000 during the ten year life of NRAS, and government backed.

I personally believe that NRAS is one of the best asset classes available at the moment. As NRAS was originally limited to 50,000 licenses over 5 different stages, not all properties are eligible for an NRAS grant; they need to be applied for. As the government didn't want to deal with 50,000 individual purchasers they assigned 'approved participants' which hold the licenses and allocate them to developments on a needs basis. This is in accordance with the strict criteria of the government which is targeting areas with the greatest need based on current and forecast rental shortages and rising rentals or exorbitant rents; so as to provide the most benefit to the community. What is the downside I hear you ask? Unfortunately as NRAS properties are such good investments that are backed by the Government for a period of ten years making them positive cash flow some developers and promoters see this as an opportunity to make larger profits by putting a premium on the sale price, therefore some don't stack up as good as others. I try and source the properties that are the best on the market with the greatest potential for capital growth as well as ideally, but not always the case, positive cash flow from day 1 with 100% finance.

I have found some fantastic properties and I can use one that I have purchased myself as an example. My approved participant was Ethan Affordable Housing. I bought a duplex, which is one block of land with two houses on it, in White

Hills, Bendigo for $585,000 turnkey. This means that everything is completed for me and I don't have to worry about a thing, the tenants can move straight in.

The back house is a 3 bedroom property and the front house is a 4 bedroom property. They rent for $230 and $260 respectively after the NRAS discount. Then as there are two properties the government don't just give me one incentive, I get two incentives! This provides $19,762 worth of tax free income per year.

I discounted my rent by $6,500 per year over both properties and I received $19,762 worth of tax free income per year from the Government. It was a no brainer for me! If you are an investor that is not keen on Bendigo or regional areas, not to worry, as Ethan Affordable Housing have product not just in Bendigo or Victoria, but have stock all over Australia as well.

As you would be aware by now Robert Kiyosaki has had a fairly big influence on both what my parents and I have achieved in property and he is of course a big advocate of property that is backed by the government. I love the following quote by Robert,

Assets put money in your pocket without you working, and liabilities take money from your pocket, even when you're working.

— *Robert Kiyosaki; Rich Dad's Conspiracy of The Rich*

THE MONEY SECRET

CHAPTER 10
TARGETING A PROPERTY

Now that you have a better understanding of the difference between purchasing a property simply for capital growth or if you also want cash flow, we can touch on finding a property.

So what does a good capital growth property look like? This is where we need to look for high capital growth areas which have a proven 10% or more capital growth over a 10 year period or more. You should concentrate on only 3 areas which all have an average growth of 10% or more over a long period of time, i.e. at least 10 years. When you have these suburbs then you need to locate the best three streets in the area and concentrate your search around them. Alternatively, locating a property that is in an undeveloped street can also be beneficial. When the rest of the street begin catching up to this area then you are guaranteed capital growth as all these new, modern buildings are built around you.

With all the new developments and money being spent by the government into certain growth areas around the major cities, there are lots of new suburbs being created. If you want to target a particular area that is better than another one, you can look at the socio economic state of that particular suburb. You do this by comparing the average income per household and you can compare that to the well known 'blue-chip' suburbs to see the difference. The more income that is in that particular area, the more likely it is that you have a good investment as people will move there and prices will go up.

Once you have found the area and property that you like, you need to make sure that emotion doesn't creep into your decision making. You need to choose what is appropriate to build for that area and build what the prospective tenants will need not what your dream home might look like. There is a saying 'give the people what they want' and 'the customer is always right'. This is no different in property; in fact it should be more important because of the larger amounts of money that you are paying for the product.

If you do a little bit of research you will hear about what is happening to the property markets in the major cities around Australia. You might hear that the Melbourne market is going down and the Sydney market is going up, or Brisbane is going down and Melbourne is going up, whatever it might be. This means that all around Australia there is a property cycle happening that you can take advantage of, if you are happy to invest in different areas.

Recently a survey was conducted asking people which areas they believed to have the highest capital growth potential and the results were as followed.

The areas they believed would get the best capital growth were:

1st: CBD Suburbs
2nd: Sea Change Locations
3rd: Outer City Suburbs
4th: Regional Centres

It might surprise you to find that the correct answers were completely the opposite as provided by Residex who are property statistics experts.

Actual best performing areas for capital growth:

1st: Regional Centres
2nd: Outer City Suburbs
3rd: Sea Change Locations
4th: CBD Suburbs

This is an interesting result and reminds us to take the emotion out of investing and purchase based on the numbers, needs, wants and demographic of the people living in the area. Remember it's an investment property, you will not be living in it, your tenants will and you therefore, you need to provide what they want not what you want.

In order to get the most out of your property investing you should also look at the timing of your purchase in respect of where the property market is in the area that you have chosen to invest in. Property markets go through cycles and these cycles can vary from state to state, city to city and even suburb to suburb and therefore, you should be prepared to look at various locations and not just properties within you own backyard or neighbourhood. What this means is that if you want to do property investing in a city that isn't at the right time of the market, you can move to another city that is at the right time of the market. This would mean that you need to feel comfortable with the investment choice buying in a city that you don't live in. For some investors it might be tough for them to get their head around the fact that regional towns are in fact a good investment choice.

Both these investment choices would probably be outside most people's comfort zone and also outside your emotion. These two reasons incorporate the reasons for people not being rich and the fear that they have for not investing. When you are investing it is all about the numbers. If you are making money, does it really matter where the property is or what colour the wall tiles are?

To assist with this decision in the property industry there is a thing called the property clock which is merely an indicator as to where the property market is at any given time. For example 12 o'clock we are at the top of the property cycle where prices are the highest and this is a good time to sell and or refinance. At 3 o'clock we are in a declining market. At 6 o'clock we are at the bottom of the market and investors should be getting ready to buy as soon as there are some signs that the market is starting to move back up again, such as short supply of properties, high clearance rates, prices starting to move up. Therefore, all these would trigger a buy situation as the clock gets to around 7 o'clock. Then of course as the market hots up again we head to 12 o'clock again where everything is overpriced and we have completed a full property cycle. Traditionally this occurs approximately every seven years and at the time of writing Melbourne, Canberra, Hobart and Adelaide are about 3 o'clock, Brisbane 6 o'clock, Sydney 5 o'clock, Perth at 7 o'clock and Darwin also at 5 o'clock.

What to look for when purchasing in the inner city suburbs:

1. Each area should have a 'life style centre' with cafes, bars, restaurants, sports centres, private schools, universities and parkland.

2. Choose 'spill-over' streets and suburbs close to established 'Blue Chip' suburbs. These suburbs have

dramatic rise in capital growth when their blue-chip neighbour becomes unaffordable in terms of equity, debt capacity and rental capacity.

3. Target streets and suburbs with established housing stock. The highest prices are always achieved in streets and suburbs which contain less 'high-rise' apartment developments.

4. Target suburbs and streets which contain private schools. For safety reasons 'wealthy' families do not want their children to travel 'too far' to get to school...especially 'rich' overseas investors.

   For example when we purchased in Balwyn and North Balwyn, all of our properties were in the Balwyn High School Zone. Balwyn High School was and is the second best public school in Victoria only behind Melbourne High where you have to sit an entrance exam to get in. Whilst this is not a private school, it is as good as and the premium to get into the Balwyn High School Zone is very high.

5. Target gay areas. Buyers and tenants have a high disposable and steady income and no children.

6. Select properties which are close to public transport

   This is not to say that if it is next to public transport it will go up in value or if it's not it won't go up in value. Balwyn doesn't have the greatest public transport as there isn't a train near it, yet it still has had significant capital growth over many years.

   Being close to public transport helps as many tenants do not have a car or they don't have a car for each person therefore require public transport to get around.

What to look for when purchasing in the outer city suburbs:

1. Only purchase properties in outer areas with an established 'entertainment' infrastructure where younger people under 40 years of age want to live: cafes, bars, restaurants, sports centres, kindergartens, schools, universities, and parkland.

2. Proximity to major shopping centres and public transport is a must.

3. Proximity to 'water' (lakes, rivers, ocean) and golf courses is a massive advantage.

4. Choose suburbs and areas which contain Brand New subdivisions and examples of opulent brand new housing of $500,000+. You want to purchase property in streets and suburbs where 'wealthier' home owners want to live.

5. Purchase property in 'beautiful' looking subdivisions, which are not more than 5 years old.

6. The best areas are the ones 'right on the beach' or in very close proximity to beaches.

   The best example I can think of for this is the Mornington Peninsula in Melbourne. This area has boomed in the last 10 years and if you got in at the start this is has been a very worthwhile investment. It might be worth while looking at investing in the other side of the bay as the entry price for the Peninsula side is beginning to be only for the high rollers.

7. Make sure the suburb or area has a rental vacancy rate of under 4%.

   There are now websites that you can find the vacancy rate for a particular suburb. However, if you want to get a personal understanding of what is happening go and visit all the real estate agents in the area and you can compare what they say to the information you found on the internet to give you a more accurate picture of what is actually happening there. You must visit every single real estate agent in the area to establish the TRUE vacancy rate.

8. Target suburbs with 'limited' sub divisional activity or where the developer is 'Blue Chip' with a long history of successful capital growth based PRICE CONTROLLED developments.

What to look for when purchasing apartments:

As you know I am not the biggest fan of purchasing apartments. If you do go down that particular track you need to make sure that you are getting the best deal that you can.

1 bedroom apartments should be 55-60 sq m which is becoming increasing more difficult to find in Melbourne. It must have 1 secured car park space and the main bedroom must be a minimum of 4m x 3.5m in size.

2 to 3 bedroom apartments should be 85-110 sq m with 2 separate bathroom/shower areas. It must have 1-2 secured car parking spaces.

The further away from the city you go the bigger the properties need to be to get any decent value in it. Once you get outside 15km from the CBD do not purchase apartments at all.

Select properties that are located within smaller low rise "boutique" style projects.

Apartments in large developments (50 units +) perform badly compared to smaller developments.

What to look for when Purchasing Townhouses:

Townhouses should be 3 bedroom, 130-150 sq. m. with an ensuite and a separate bathroom/shower area; it must have a 1-2 car garage or an extra 'open' car space.

Townhouses are the most popular and in-demand properties favoured by the under 40 years of age population. Most Australians do not want the hassle of home maintenance but still want all the space, privacy and entertainment advantages of living in a house. It is because of this reason that I am a big fan of townhouses and I believe this is the smallest that you should go if you are looking at buying.

Townhouses also offer the best 'bang for buck' value of all inner city properties due to their lower 'domestic' construction costs. It could cost three times more money to build the same 'space and quality' apartment as it does a townhouse.

Apartments can cost $3,000 per sq. m. to build whilst similar quality townhouses can cost only $1,000 per sq. m. to build.

The further out from the city you go to purchase, think about only purchasing established second-hand properties for refurbishment purposes.

The best properties to purchase for refurbishment are larger apartments with high ceilings (2.7m+) in the best blue-chip areas with brand new 'expensive' developments in close proximity.

What to do when purchasing the property for solely capital growth benefits

1. Choose properties which have been on the market for at least 2 months. The real estate agent and <u>most importantly</u> the vendor are a lot more desperate if the property hasn't sold after 2 months of marketing.

2. Never offer to purchase a property before auction, only after the auction FAILED and the property has been 'passed-in'.

You should do those things unless you find a very good deal straight away that might not fit all the above criteria and you believe it is a steal. If not follow the above rules.

If the property has been on the market for a while then both the vendor and agent are desperate to sell the property. This means that emotion comes into it and you are more likely to get it for a better price. The agent's commission is virtually the same if the agent sells for the list price (vendor's asking price) or 5% to 10% less and the agent wants to move onto their next property.

It's better to get something rather than nothing. If there is no sale, there is no commission, and all the time spent on selling the property has been in vain. The agent does not get paid any more money for the extra time they spend selling the property. The vendor also gets a bit worried if he hasn't sold the property yet. It is starting to cost the vendor more money on marketing. They are still paying interest on the property and it just costing them money each week and they still have other costs like rates and property taxes.

The longer it is on the market means the agent might start losing motivation and just move onto their next property where they might have a better chance of selling it.

As you can see there are lots of benefits to getting a property that has been on the market for a while and getting it at a good price.

CHAPTER 11
PRINCIPAL & INTEREST OR
INTEREST ONLY

This is an area where a lot of people go wrong and can lose significant amounts of money as opposed to making significant amounts of money. This, in my opinion, is the easiest way to turn someone from being poor into someone that is rich. Where people go wrong is that they are taught from a very young age to pay off their home loan as quick as they can, and believe that this is what Principal and Interest repayments are going to do for them. What they forget to realise is that they are paying significantly more to do this per week, per month and per year as the money is mainly going towards the interest in the first few years anyway. Whereas, if they were paying **Interest Only** then they would have more cash flow and as 'cash flow is king' it could be possible for them to invest in another property.

With a second property they could utilise the positive cash flow from that property to pay down the Principal portion on the original property or even utilise the capital growth by selling the investment property. Switching to Interest Only saves them a lot of cash flow and still gives them the option to pay off their home loan if they so choose as opposed to paying Principal and Interest and paying down the lots of interest at the beginning of the loan.

So the easiest way to demonstrate the difference in repayments and where your money is going is to show you the difference between Principal & Interest (P&I) and Interest Only (IO). As Melbourne's medium house price is nearly $600,000 at the moment lets use 90% of that which is $540,000. Interest rates in Australia at the time of writing this section were about 7%.

P&I Weekly Repayments = $829
IO Weekly Repayments = $727

So the difference per year by paying Interest Only on this amount is $5,304. This is $5,304 in your bank account compounding interest and that you can use for investment purposes. Add another $5,408 from purchasing a positive cash flowed property then this is over $10,000 of your hard earned cash that you are saving per year whereas the less educated investors are spending this money.

So if that isn't enough to show you how that is a huge difference, by paying Principal & Interest we have one house that is growing in value earning us capital growth which we will repay in 30 years time. However, by paying Interest Only in three years time we have enough money to buy another investment property by leveraging your money. So now we will have two properties both growing in value earning us capital growth and the investment property providing us positive cash flow in only three years! Alternatively you can continue to pay Principal & Interest and pay off your house in 30 years time as that is the period of time in which your loan is calculated.

So now, if you have two properties that are doing this do you think that after a while if you wanted to you could take out the equity from one of them and pay out the other, or alternatively use the income that you are receiving and use that to build up enough for a deposit to buy another one. Think of how much wealthier you would be if you bought an investment property every three years, that's 10 properties as opposed to 1 paying Principal & Interest over a 30 year loan term all by changing the type of repayments that you make.

CHAPTER 12
LEVERAGE

A common question I have is that people don't understand what a deposit is and how much money they require to purchase a house or an investment property. Another thing I often get asked when explaining to people the dollar amounts of purchasing and investing in property is, 'how long will it take to get my money back?'. The answer is it all depends on your strategy and the property market. It is impossible to accurately predict the exact time line.

Property should be treated like a business. The idea of property is to get your money back out as fast as you can. Wealth creation is all about the speed of money. The sooner you can get it back the sooner you can invest in another investment property.

If you purchase a property worth $300,000 and you put $15,000 of your own funds into the property you will owe the bank $275,000. That $15,000 that you invested is not gone; it is still your money as you have just invested it. So if you decide to sell the property and it is still worth $300,000 then you pay the bank back their $275,000 and you get to keep your $15,000. But if the property goes up to $350,000 then you still owe the bank $275,000 and you have just made $50,000 for only putting in $15,000 which is a 333% return on your money.

At this point you can go back to the bank and increase the size of your loan and take out your $15,000 that you originally invested out of your personal savings. You could even ask for a bigger loan depending on the bank lending criteria, and then it is possible that you may have none of your own money left in the deal and you may have surplus funds. All sound well and good but I also get asked can you actually lose money in property? The answer to that is yes. Property goes in cycles and is a long term investment so if you buy at the top of the market and go to sell at the bottom of the market you may lose money and that is why before purchasing anything you need to do research and due diligence to reduce the prospect of losing when buying. There is a saying in property that goes, "you make your money in real estate when you buy not when you sell". What this means is do your research, know your worst case scenario and buy right and you will make money in the long term.

Almost everyone that you speak to that is rich believes in using other people's money (OPM) to make themselves rich, this is called leverage. If you are not using your own money it is a lot easier to make money.

Another common misconception people have about deposits and buying houses is that you need to have a 10% deposit for the real estate agent and a total of 20% for a deposit for the bank to consider financing a loan. This used to be the case but nowadays everything is negotiable with the vendor. With the banks the amount of deposit required depends on the type of lender that you go to and the type of employment that you are in. In most cases you should be able to borrow 95% of the purchase price, also known as Loan to Value Ratio (LVR) which means you only need 5% of the purchase price as a deposit and the bank will lend you the rest; i.e. the other 95%. However, this depends on that banks lending policy at that particular time as their policies are subject to change. That being said, it is also important to realise that there are other costs, which also add up to about 5% of the purchase price, such as the loan establishment fee, lenders mortgage insurance, legal fees stamp duty etc. which need to be funded by the purchaser, when you buy a property, as the bank will not fund you for these costs. What this means now is that if you were originally going to put 20% in then you could effectively now purchase 2 to 4 times the amount of property provided that you have the serviceability to repay the loan and the cash for the fees and charges. Therefore, you can now purchase 4 properties instead of one; you may be beginning to appreciate the power of leverage. You are now making four times the amount of money; four times the capital growth and four times the cash flow all with the same amount of money and you are effectively using other people's money.

Now that you are aware that we need a lot less money to get into property than you thought, let's see how leveraging can really make you wealthy. I just showed you an example of how leveraging your money provides you with massive returns. Let's stem on from that example a little further and imagine you are actually purchasing a $300,000 property. You go to your finance broker and say you have a 5% deposit on a $300,000 house which is $15,000 and would like a 95% loan ($285,000) to complete the purchase. Your finance broker looks around and gets you a loan that best suits you. Then you buy the property and wait. So you have spent $15,000 of your own money. The rule of property is that it doubles every 7-10 years, let's be conservative and say that your property will double in 12 years which is a growth rate of 6%. So in one year your $300,000 property is now worth $318,000, so you have already made more than 100% on your money in year 1.

Let's say you decided to sell the property after 5 years. Assuming a straight line growth rate of 6% your property is now worth $401,468. You still owe the bank $285,000 as you were paying interest only. This leaves you with a profit of $116,468. Then we need to take away selling costs of approximately $20,000 leaving you with a before tax profit of $91,468 which is an average return of $18,294 per annum or as a percentage of your money invested, your cash on cash return is 121% per annum return on your investment in just five years! Or alternatively you can leave your money in a savings account earning you about 4% per annum.

It is very important to master the concept of increasing your equity i.e. your net worth, over time as opposed to exclusively focusing on reducing your borrowings. A lot of people are not happy to have debt and simply focus on the amount of debt that they have rather than the income and capital growth/equity that they are receiving from having that debt and the wealth that they are creating by having their money leveraged.

To me there are two different types of debt. The first one is good debt, which is debt that makes you money. This is used for the purchase of an income producing investments which puts money in your pocket. The second type of debt is consumer debt, or what I call bad debt which is debt that sends you broke and takes money out of your pocket which is used for such things like Big Screen TV's, holidays, boats and other items which are depreciating assets and do not make you money. I like good debt, I do not like bad debt.

As I have already given you an example of how good debt and using other people's money (OPM) can be beneficial for you, let me show you another example of how property can make you very wealthy. This is what I call my 7-10 year financial freedom or retirement plan and why I work because I choose to and not because I have to.

In year 1 you purchase a positive cash flowed investment property worth $300,000. You know I love good debt and we want to use none of our own money so you have a 100% loan on this property. Therefore you now owe $300,000 to the lender and you pay Interest Only repayments therefore you do not pay $1 dollar off your loan, never reducing the 100% that you owe. I simply just repay the interest. Now as this property is positive cash flow the income that you receive from the property is more than the interest that you are paying and covers all of the other costs associated with the property such as rates and real estate agent's commission.

In year 2 you purchase your second positively cash flowed investment property also worth $300,000 and you employ the same tactic with 100% finance. You still owe $300,000 on the first property that you purchased and you now owe 100% on the second property as well which totals $600,000.

In year 3 you purchase your third investment property. Yes, you guessed it we are going to use the same method and use 100% finance. So you still owe $300,000 on property 1, $300,000 on property 2 and now $300,000 on property 3 just paying Interest Only.

Now you might think, but I owe $900,000. Yes, buy you are also receiving income for having this $900,000 debt.

So in years 4-10 you do exactly the same thing that you did with the first 3 properties continuing to pay interest only, never paying $1 off your loan. So in year 11 you owe 3 million to the bank, however, what has happened to property number one? Has it gone up in value? Yes, it has as property doubles every 7-10 years. So property number 1 is now worth $600,000. But how much do we owe the bank? If you remember it was $300,000? So what would happen if we then sold this property would we receive a $300,000 profit? Yes we would! So do you think you could live off $300,000 a year?

So in year 12 you have 9 properties, what happened to property number 2 that you bought? This is now worth $600,000 as well but you only owe the bank $300,000. So can I sell this property and also make a $300,000 profit? Absolutely!

In year 13 property number 3 is worth $600,000 and you owe the bank $300,000. You can sell the property and make $300,000. This is why I say it's a 7-10 year retirement plan depending on how much income you want to have and how quickly the properties double. Of course you don't have to sell the properties in year 11 and 12 or sell one a year, you can hold on to them if you would like and live off the positive cash flow, it really depends on your personal preference and the situation you find yourself in. Another option is to refinance just one of the properties for example property number 1 is now worth an estimated $600,000 and based on the bank lending you say 80% of its value you could now borrow $480,000 of which you still owe the bank $300,000 and the balance of $180,000 you can use for whatever you like. If you are conservative like my mum and don't like a very large 'good debt' you can sell five and pay down the debt on the other five and keep them debt free. These concepts just show you that you don't have to work 9-5 your whole life - there are other ways. I see property as a vehicle to do this.

So to show you how refinancing your property would work in year 11 with property number one I have made up a table to demonstrate:

What if you knew with absolute certainty you could do this?

Year		Income		Income	
1:	$300,000	Year 11:	$180,000	Year 21:	$480,000
2:	$300,000	Year 12:	$180,000	Year 22:	$480,000
3:	$300,000	Year 13:	$180,000	Year 23:	$480,000
4:	$300,000	Year 14:	$180,000	Year 24:	$480,000
5:	$300,000	Year 15:	$180,000	Year 25:	$480,000
6:	$300,000	Year 16:	$180,000	Year 26:	$480,000
7:	$300,000	Year 17:	$180,000	Year 27:	$480,000
8:	$300,000	Year 18:	$180,000	Year 28:	$480,000
9:	$300,000	Year 19:	$180,000	Year 29:	$480,000
10:	$300,000	Year 20:	$180,000	Year 30:	$480,000

Now just to explain the last column as you might be a little bit confused. The property doubled in 10 years to $600,000, so in another 10 years the property will double again to $1,200,000. If you refinance the property to 80% you now have a $960,000 loan but only owe the bank $480,000 leaving you with $480,000 left over to spend for yourself.

One thing to remember is how much of your own money did you actually use? You were borrowing 100% of the funds all the time and yet you still don't have to work at all if you don't want to, using none of your own money. I hope this shows you the power of leverage and using other people's money and also the fact that it doesn't matter how much debt you find yourself in, it's the position that the debt puts you in. In this case debt is very good so you shouldn't be afraid of how much debt you have. This is a whole other perspective of debt that successful people are using, and there's no reason why it can't be used to your advantage as well.

Quiz:

Do you currently have an investment property with a loan?

How much are you prepared to leverage your money to make you wealthy?

If this plan looks appealing to you and you need assistance to 'work because you want to and not because you have to?' Then get in touch with us and go to our website as we are here to help.

http://www.moneysecretsthatwork.com

CHAPTER 13
SELF MANAGED SUPER FUNDS (SMSF)

I feel it is important to put this chapter under leverage, as it is only now that people are starting to catch on that managed super funds are not providing you very good returns and lots of people are losing a lot of money having their money tied up in these sorts of accounts. The Australian Prudential Regulation Authority (APRA) recently revealed that the Australian superannuation industry lost $18.5 billion of their clients' money in the last financial year. Having a managed super fund is not the only way!

Self Managed Super Funds have been around for a long time, it has only been recently that you have been able to borrow in your SMSF which enables you to leverage into such investments as property. (Note: to set up a SMSF so that it can borrow is a specific process as is managing your own fund and therefore, you will need to seek professional assistance in doing this but in my opinion it is well worth it. You need to be careful when setting up a SMSF as some organisations can charge up to $16,000 - $20,000 but you should be able to do the whole process for under $5,000 so be careful and do your research)

By way of example I will demonstrate why I believe a SMSF for investing in property is one of the best ways to ensure your financial security in retirement. Let's say you have $60,000 already in your SMSF and you have a $10,000 contribution every year. You borrow money in your super fund (currently the most you can borrow is 80% of the value of the property) and you purchase a property worth $300,000.

All the property has to do is go up by the value which property goes up every year, say a conservative 7.2% which would give you a $21,600 increase on the property. This is also a 36% return on your money (the $60,000 deposit) in year 1. You would be very lucky to earn 5% in managed super funds these days, in fact you would be lucky if your super fund went up at all.

In year 2 your property goes up another 7.2% or $23,155 meaning you have now made $44,755 and only invested $60,000. This is a 74.5% return on your money only after 2 years. In year 3 you make another $24,822 meaning you have now made $69,577 and only invested $60,000. Pretty impressive! Therefore in only 3 years you have now made 116% on your money!

Please be aware that there are no guarantees you will get these returns, however, we know history always repeats itself and long term property in Australia has always grown at least 7.2% over a ten year period so you are putting the odds in your favour by investing your superannuation in property. However, this of course is only half the story as you can go out and find positive cash flow properties as well. You can put these positive cash flowed properties into your SMSF and then not only would you be getting capital growth from your investment; you would also be getting money into your SMSF each week from the investment property. What an excellent strategy to adopt positive cash flow each week and capital growth long term. This is something that has not been occurring in the industry with managed super funds.

This is a prime example of how leverage works and using someone else's money. So ask yourself, why would I have my money in an industry super fund where I am just losing money every year, when I can set up my own SMSF, manage it myself and buy property by leveraging my super fund money? (Tip: a self managed superfund can have up to four members and therefore, it is possible to partner with three other people to obtain sufficient funds to raise the deposit to get started.)

Quiz:

Do you know where all your super money is?

Do you know how much you have in your super account/s?

Do you know how much return are you getting from your super fund per annum?

Have you heard of a Self Managed Super Fund (SMSF)?

Do you think you would get a higher return from a SMSF?

Are you now going to invest in a SMSF?

Need assistance to set up a SMSF for lower prices and learn how to 'work because you want to and not because you have to?' Then get in touch with us and go to our website as we are here to help.

http://www.moneysecretsthatwork.com

CHAPTER 14
BUYING IN 'UP' OR 'DOWN' MARKETS

The property market has two sides, it has the top of the market (this is when all the property prices are very high) and it has the bottom of the market (this is when property prices are very low). Property goes up and down each day, each month and each year, therefore, the market is changing all the time. So with this in mind when is the right time to buy property?

Some people have the perception that the best time to buy is when the property is at the bottom of the market. While this may be a good idea, other people don't really care when they buy property. Then, there is the theory that some subscribe to, which is, it doesn't matter when you buy or sell property as long as you are doing it in the same market.

How often when you talk to people about property and buying housing and house prices do you hear them say that the property prices are too expensive to buy anything at the moment and that you shouldn't buy and you should wait for the prices to drop? They tell you to buy when the prices are down or 'at the bottom'. There are both positives and negatives to buying when the market is at the top or when the market is at the bottom.

The problem with buying when the market is low or at the bottom is that the valuations don't usually stack up. By this I mean that in order to make money you need to use other people's money; I take you back to the term, leverage that was in Chapter 12. So in order to use other people's money you need to borrow money from the bank or obtain money from investors. As most people are familiar with borrowing money from the bank we shall use that as an example. When you borrow money from the bank they value the property and then you get a Loan to Value Ratio (LVR). If you purchase a property for $300,000 this is how much you have agreed to pay the vendor (seller) for his property. So when you go to the bank they very rarely give you 100% finance so you apply for a 90% loan, this means that you want to try and borrow $270,000 from the bank. When the bank value the property they decide that although you agreed to pay the seller $300,000 at the current time they believe that the property is only worth $280,000. The bank will now only give you 90% of the 280,000 so now they will give you $252,000 which is $18,000 less than what you were originally applying for.

As you have already agreed to pay the vendor $300,000 he still wants that amount. This means that in order to purchase this property you now need to find an extra $18,000 on top of the $30,000 that you were originally investing in the purchase. That is 60% more than what you have already put in!

If this still doesn't sound like much to you, then, consider this:

That $18,000 was potentially a 5% deposit on another property worth $360,000. That property only has to go up to $378,000 in value before you have made 100% on your deposit money! However, because you bought at the wrong time of the market, in a down market, the valuation does not come back at the purchase price and, therefore, you can only purchase one property and not two. You could have had 2 properties instead of 1 working for you, however, because the bank backed valuation came in lower; because you bought a property at the bottom of the market, you are only able to buy one property. The difference between buying one property and buying two properties over the long term would be massive regarding your wealth as if you managed to buy two, both properties would be achieving capital growth. Therefore, for the same amount of deposit money you would be getting twice the amount of leverage, cash flow and capital growth.

So now let's consider you are buying that same property when it is at the top of the market, that means the price is at the higher end and more expensive. Instead of purchasing the property for $300,000 it is now worth $320,000 which is a 6.6% increase in the price also a $40,000 difference in bank value. So when you go to the bank and ask for 90% LVR the valuation will come in at $320,000 because the property is at the top of the market. What this means is that you only have to put $32,000 which is the 10% of the purchase price which is considerably less than the $48,000 that you have to put in when the property is at the bottom of the market.

Although we haven't discussed property development yet (to be covered in a later chapter), it is important to note that it can be beneficial to buy when the market is down if you intend on developing the land as opposed to buying in boom times when the market price is high. That is a different strategy.

During boom times development sites are harder to find, are often overpriced and often have to be purchased without suitable contract conditions. Development approvals take longer to obtain, building prices increase and interest rate rises are a strong possibility as the regulators try to take the heat out of the market.

When the market is down you have more negotiating power with the vendor as when the property market is at, or near the bottom, there are less buyers and properties usually take a lot longer to sell, leading to desperate sellers. This allows you to control the terms of the deal. There are also greater opportunities to purchase using an option. This is where you control the property but do not settle on if for a long period of time (say twelve or eighteen months) which gives you time to get things such as planning permits and presales organised prior to settling and not having to pay holding costs such as interest and rates. You might also be able to negotiate a delayed settlement as far as you like or do a Joint Venture (JV) with the seller so that it is a win-win situation. It gives you more room to move and more opportunity to make money. The down side, however, is that it is usually more difficult to get financing from the bank which means you need to be more creative with your financing strategies.

Quiz:

What have you been taught in regard to buying in up and down markets?

Do you now understand that buying at the bottom of the market is not necessarily the best option to become wealthy?

Need assistance so that you can 'work because you want to and not because you have to?' Then get in touch with us and go to our website as we are here to help.

http://www.moneysecretsthatwork.com

CHAPTER 15
LAND VS. APARTMENT

When you are purchasing property you need to think what you are purchasing it for and what type of property you are going to buy. I find so many first home buyers as well as people looking to invest are now buying apartments. A number of reasons exist for this, it may be that they are attracted by the lower price, they just want to get into the market or they want to purchase close to the CBD and so feel that apartments are their entry.

People purchase property for their shelter and so that they can say that they have achieved the Australian dream of owning their own home. Apart from this reason there are only two reasons for purchasing investment properties. Firstly it is to gain access to capital growth (increase your wealth) and secondly to receive rental income (increase your cash flow or tax deductibility). As an important starting point, **never ever, ever** buy a property solely based on getting a tax deduction. The reason you buy property is for capital growth and cash flow, and any tax deduction should be seen as a bonus.

So when purchasing property it is important to understand whether you are buying it simply to increase your wealth, to give you extra income, to provide you with tax deductions or a combination of all of them. Your net worth will appreciate over time due to the capital appreciation of the property and this will make you wealthy, as it is the capital growth and not the income that makes you wealthy. In order to do this you need to pick your property wisely. Capital growth will relate to the land, as this is what appreciates over time and is influenced heavily by supply. For example, it is impossible to add more land to the Central Business District (CBD) of Melbourne; however, it is very easy to 'build up' into the air space in Melbourne. So, what is more valuable the land or the buildings? If you purchase the right land, then, over time it becomes worth more and more and therefore, more valuable.

You would simply only purchase an apartment for its location. The size of the apartments can be small, there is no land value (well very little land value) and there are lots and lots more apartments. Let's take a quick look at what happens. One year the latest and greatest apartments are built and you think 'Oh wow! That's amazing!'. By then the next year the new and improved latest and greatest apartment is built and your apartment is super seeded. It is now no longer the 'wow' and 'amazing' apartment that it used to be. Over time apartments are also not as good value for money. They very quickly become outdated and outclassed. There is another saying within the property circle and that is that 'land appreciates and buildings depreciate.' I am not saying that buying apartments are not a good investment as they might be producing you good cash flow which may be what you're after, however, they may not appreciate the same as what something with more substance and land will. At least if you buy a house or a townhouse, the property is a little bit bigger, has more value and are not as readily outdated.

The best example I can think of to demonstrate the difference between houses and apartments is one of the purchases that my dad made. Back about 12 years ago now when dad and one of his friends both bought property around about the same time, Dad bought a block of land in

Belmore Road, Balwyn for $287,000. It was a derelict old house on a large block of land, nothing special. His mate (let's call him Steve), bought a brand new apartment in the Melbourne CBD in a high-rise building for around about $220,000. So let's compare the two locations, one is in the heart and soul of Melbourne's CBD right next to Southern Cross Station. The other one is in a little suburb called Balwyn which is 11km from Melbourne CBD in the inner eastern suburbs. So just think to yourself, which deal you would have bought with this little information that I have just provided?

Let's compare how much the two purchases are worth today. My dad demolished the old derelict home that was there and built a new $350,000 house on it. This would make his total investment so far $637,000. He then sold the property 10 years later for 1.6 million dollars taking a profit of $963,000. In comparison, Steve's apartment in the heart of Melbourne would be lucky to be worth $400,000 in today's market as the number of apartments in the CBD have increased dramatically over the years and so now the older ones are finding it difficult to achieve good valuations. Whilst the Balwyn property has doubled and nearly doubled again, this apartment hasn't even doubled once and yet we are 12 years on.

Even if my dad hadn't developed the land by building a new house of it, the land still would have appreciated over time. For example the property next door which was pure land value sold for just under 1 million dollars. So in the 10 years that my dad owned this property it went from $287,000 to just under 1 million dollars! That's an increase of around

$700,000 in 10 years, or equivalent to $70,000 per year. Alternatively you can buy the brand new apartment in Melbourne for $220,000 and make $180,000 in 12 years. It's your call.

Now some of you might be thinking 'but the apartment would have had high rent and could have been positive cash flow.' Let's just assume that it was positive cash flow and he was earning $100 per week from this property week in, week out for 10 years. This equates to $52,000 that he would have made. How much of a better investment does that positive cash flow make it compared to buying the land? It is good to purchase a positively cash flowed investment property, however, Belmore Road also had positive cash flow and it received much high capital growth!

DEPRECIATION

I've added this little sub heading in here as it I think it is important to touch on.

So firstly for those of you who are not really clear on what depreciation is:

Depreciation is a non-cash expense that reduces the value of an asset as a result of wear and tear, age, or obsolescence. Most assets lose their value over time (in other words, they depreciate), and must be replaced once the end of their useful life is reached. There are several accounting methods that are used in order to write off an asset's depreciation cost over the period of its useful life. Because it is a non-cash expense, and the Australian Taxation Office (ATO) allows us to claim depreciation on our properties that are used for investment purposes. The depreciation claimed, in accordance with accounting and ATO guidelines can reduce our taxable income and increase the cash flow from an investment property.

Here is an example of where I had a client once ask me if it were better to buy one house for $800,000 or to buy two houses for $400,000 for the best depreciation results. I thought this was a very interesting question as that was what she was interested in and that was her reason for buying an investment property; depreciation!

So, what is better, and how do you get the benefits of depreciation? Firstly, you need to be aware that land appreciates whereas buildings depreciate as they get older. It is the same with cars - the more you use them the less valuable they become and the more in price they go down. So if you own an investment property and each year the value of your building is effectively going down, then you are eligible for a tax benefit as you are technically losing money on your investment.

Obviously you can't claim the whole building amount in your first year and then sell it. The rule is you can claim 2.5% of the building cost per year, so this will last for 40 years until your building is effectively worth nothing. You can also claim on the fixtures and fittings that are in the house as well and this is calculated at approximately 15% per year depending on what calculation method your accountant uses.

So going back to our question; Is it better to buy one investment property for $800,000 or to buy two for $400,000 for depreciation benefits? There is no straight answer to this question. She needs to weigh up her reasons for purchasing the property. If she has purchased them purely for depreciation benefits then she has to determine the building costs for all three properties. For example, the $800,000 property might have a build cost of $200,000 and a land value of $600,000 meaning she would get depreciation benefits on the $200,000. The $400,000 property might have a build cost of $200,000 and a land value of $200,000 meaning she would get the same depreciation benefits for both properties, but could purchase two $400,000 properties for the same price and get double the depreciation benefits. So find out what the construction cost is of the building and what year it is to determine the amount that you can claim on depreciation. Remember you cannot claim depreciation on the land value, only the original construction value.

Quiz:

What are your reasons for purchasing an investment property?

Does land become more or less valuable over time?

Do buildings go up or down in value over time?

Need assistance to 'work because you want to and not because you have to?' Then get in touch with us and go to our website as we are here to help.

http://www.moneysecretsthatwork.com

CHAPTER 16
BUY BIG OR BUY SMALL

Someone sent me an article once called 'Why Australia's appetite for property is becoming smaller – and cheaper.' This article pretty much says that like small cars, small apartments are becoming more fashionable and also the choice of property. Why? Because property prices are going up and we are running out of land, small apartments are the only thing that people can afford. Out of this article I have two points that I want to touch on:

'apartments are more popular than ever before. The 2011 census confirmed they account for 14% of all dwellings, up from 11% in 2006. Apartments made better capital gains than houses over the past few years, and they're becoming a lot more affordable, too.'

Of course apartments are more popular than ever as that is what is required. It is all about supply and demand. The population of the cities is growing; therefore, we need somewhere to put the people. As we start to run out of land, it becomes more valuable. More apartments mean more supply and the less land that is out there. I will use Melbourne as an example since that's where I'm from, the government have picked the growth corridors which is the northern and western areas as they have not previously developed those areas for residential purposes. They are building lots of new estates out there, but how many of them will be apartments? Who wants to live in an apartment 50km away from the city? I know I don't. The reason apartments have increased in popularity is that people need somewhere closer to the city to live in that they can afford.

House prices go up and down in value all the time, as do apartment values. Prices don't constantly rise but they have an average of 9.2% growth rate around the country. This doesn't mean that without fail prices will rise 9.2% each year, it means over a period of time property value goes up by an average of 9.2% each year. This means that it might have years of 0% growth and negative growth, but then we have boom years. House prices reaching the top of the market also has a direct correlation to the banks and how much money they are lending and their lending policies. We will touch on that a bit later on in the Finance section.

The second point is:

'In real estate, big homes have been on the nose for a few years. They're a lot more expensive, and they cost a lot more to run and maintain. In 2011, only 1% of sales across Australia were for properties over $1 million, so big and expensive homes are a very small segment of the market.'

I personally love this statement as this demonstrates how good it is to hold land, lots of it and also big homes. Again it is all reliant on the principle of supply and demand. If you are in the 1% of people that have it then you are laughing as it is such a small section of the market. This means that the supply is very low, meaning the prices eventually have to go up as there is not much of it. Yes it is a lot more expensive and not everyone can buy it, but if you do hold it you are in a very good position as you can't just blow up land. Well you can it will just put a big hole in the ground that you will have to fill again. What I am saying is the land will always be there, however, you cannot make any more of it without incurring gigantic expense, such as the islands they are building off the coast of Dubai. On the other hand, what happens if you just own an apartment and it gets burnt down, how much value do you have left now?

Now I'm not saying that there isn't anything good about purchasing at the lower end of the market and getting a little bit of land, I'm just trying to get you thinking outside the square. You need to understand the different options that are available, find out what interests you, make yourself a plan and work to that plan.

There are lots of benefits to buying in the lower end of the market. How many people can afford a $300,000 house as opposed to a 1 million dollar house? You are opening up the market to a lot more people as everyone can always afford it.

Another downside to owning big houses can be the rental yield that you receive which is usually lower and therefore your holding costs and out of pocket expenses can be higher. This is something that you will have to weigh up against the capital growth and why I suggest to have both positive cash flow properties in your portfolio and properties that will have high capital growth. Because of the discrepancy in the rental yields on the more expensive properties my dad says, buy income producing assets and rent your lifestyle, in other words do not go out and buy a big expensive house to live in yourself, rent it instead and spend your money on assets that are going to put money into your pocket each week or achieve massive capital growth or both. There will be more on this in the next chapter.

Another issue you may have is if you buy at the upper end of the market i.e. in the top 1% over a million dollars, then those property prices are the first to decrease if you have a slip in the market. You can lose millions of dollars in a very short period of time on paper or in reality if you have to sell in a down market. A property can go from $4 million to $2 million as the only thing that determines the prices at this level is supply and demand. If lots of people want a big property in a fantastic location they will fight for it and pay the $4 million, whereas if there is nobody that wants it or cannot get the finance to buy it you may be forced to take what you can get for it and therefore it is now only worth $2 million.

A perfect example of this would be Richard Branson's purchase of Necker Island in the Caribbean. The island was on the market for $5 million, however, Richard only offered $100,000 before finally purchasing the island for $180,000. Branson estimated in 2006 that the island's value had grown to approximately $60 million, a 33,233 percent increase on what he paid for it.

It's a bit like a stock market crash. If you have property at the lower end that really doesn't get affected as much and you certainly don't lose millions of dollars in a short period of time. The higher end property on the other hand is the first to come off.

There are pros and cons to picking a strategy, depending on what you want to do. You may want to diversify and do a few in each segment; you might not be able to afford to do the higher end market so you may not have a choice. But I'm sure you have heard the term 'high risk, high reward'? This is exactly what you are doing when buying in the upper end of the market - going for a higher reward. If you make 100% on your money on $300,000 it is a lot less than making 100% of your money on $1 million but the extra benefit is that you are buying something that is low in supply.

Need assistance in picking a strategy and want to 'work because you want to and not because you have to?' Then get in touch with us and go to our website as we are here to help.

http://www.moneysecretsthatwork.com

CHAPTER 17
RENTING VS. LIVING IN YOUR OWN HOME

I'm not sure about your personal situations but through my experiences most females want to live in their own home. Why is this? Well, it is firstly the way they are wired, which causes them to crave security. It is also an emotional thing - they want to know that it's theirs and they can do whatever they want with it. They also get taught from the young age that the respectable progression includes going to school, getting a good education, a job, buying a house and paying it off as quickly as possible.

Women also like to 'nest', which means they want to paint the walls, put holes in the walls to hang stuff up and tell all their friends that they have their own home. (Security)

This is fine, but there is also another way! My family had our own home which we were living in. It was a $1 million house in Balwyn and we had mortgage repayments on it as most people do with the homes they live in. The mortgage repayments were $1,700 per week as interest rates in Australia were very high at the time (as a general rule, compared to the rest of the world our rates are very high all the time). Nevertheless a $1 million home for $1,700 per week. After deciding to move closer to the city and rent a $1 million house in Richmond, we were paying $650 dollars per week. The house was also much newer than the house in Balwyn which was comparably old and ready to be bulldozed in a heartbeat. So by renting as opposed to living in our home we save over $1,000 per week which is over $50,000 per year.

Think of what you could do with this $50,000 per year. You might decide to buy another investment property, or go on a holiday, buy a car and simply just use it as spending money. You can do all of this because you took the emotion out of living in your own home and instead decided to rent your life style! Let's say the reason was that your loving girlfriend or wife wanted to live in her own home. What if you said to her "darling, if we live in someone else's home and pay rent I will give you $50,000 a year!" How many pairs of shoes do you think she could imagine buying with that amount of money? Or you could spend 6 months of the year living in the Bahamas if you wanted to! These are the options that taking the emotion out of property does for you!

However, with the knowledge that you obtain from reading this book and actually going out and implementing some of these strategies you may find that you can afford to live in your own house if you wish. As I was growing up we kept moving from house to house and I wasn't really sure why we were doing this. We moved from one old house to another old house and when we moved out dad would bulldoze the old house and build a big new one; which he then rented out. He did this about five or six times and as it turned out each of these houses were positive cash flow after all expenses, which meant it put money into his pocket each week and he also sold a couple of the houses he built. Anyway, after he did this half a dozen times he built a new house in Balwyn North which we went and lived in. It was our family home where we lived for 5 years, which was the longest that we had stayed in any one place. It was then that I realised why we had kept on moving and living in the old houses, then building the new ones and renting them out, the positive cash flow coming in from the investment properties was paying for the new house that we were living in - effectively we were living in a big new house for free.

So yes, there are benefits to living in your own home and I am not against it as long as it is the best decision for you and you are happy to give up $50,000 extra cash a year to do so.

There is also a benefit of having a principal place of residence (living in your own home). This is another strategy that can be used to make significant amounts of money; I just wanted to make sure that we are not doing things based on emotion. When you live in your own home and have a principal place of residence, you do not pay capital gains tax when you sell it. So an example of this is when my parents built this house for us to live in when we were teenagers. This property was in North Balwyn backing onto a park. So dad bought the land for $370,000 and built on the land for $370,000 meaning he had spent $740,000. He then sold the house after we had lived in it for 5 years for $1.6 million. This is a profit of $860,000 in 5 years or $172,000 per year and is required to pay no tax on the profits, as a principal place of residence is exempt from capital gains tax. So this is one benefit to living it your own home and can be used very effectively. You need to be careful how much you chop and change houses and principal places of residence as the government has caught onto this and will monitor you more cautiously if you use this strategy too often.

Now, to finish off this story about moving out of the Balwyn property and renting I would like to share with you what happened next. Because we sold the Balwyn property that freed up mum & dad's borrowing capacity again. They were now also saving approximately $1,000 per week so they went out and bought 6 new positive cash flow properties that were producing approximately $60,000 per annum positive cash flow between them after tax. Let's review their two positions:

Living in their own home was costing them about $1,700 per week or $88,400 per annum.

By selling their home and renting, it was costing them $35,000 per annum but then there was additional income coming in of $60,000 per annum from the investment properties that will over the long term also provide capital growth – they were now living for free and pocketing a further $25,000 per annum, after tax.

In summary they went from negative $88,400 to positive $25,000 or a cash flow turnaround of $103,400 from selling one property. Ask yourself the question, what is it worth to you to live in your own home?

I would like to make a very big distinction here; we have spoken about two different strategies in regard to the principal place of residence. One was just an old house that we did nothing with and it was during a period of slow to no growth. Whereas with the property in North Balwyn that we did live in for five years where we made a lot of capital growth, it was in a rising market and the majority of the capital growth was manufactured as we bought the old house, bulldozed it and built a big new one. Had we just kept the old house the growth and return would not have been as great as we ended up achieving. So that brings us to the next chapter where we will talk about property development.

Quiz:

Is your dream to live and own your own home?

Do you have a strategy in place to achieve this?

Do you think that one of these strategies can help you achieve your goal quicker?

Need assistance in creating your plan so that you can 'work because you want to and not because you have to?' Then get in touch with us and go to our website as we are here to help.

http://www.moneysecretsthatwork.com

CHAPTER 18
PROPERTY DEVELOPMENT

As you can see from the few examples I have mentioned of what my dad did with developing properties himself, there is some serious money to be made! This is a great way to increase the value of your property and hence the equity (the bit that is yours and not the banks), from day one. People will pay a premium to not have to build the house themselves and also not have to wait the time that it takes to build a house. Because of this, you do the job for them and you get to keep the profits. You are buying a block of land and improving its value.

There are lots of different ways in which you can add value to a property and we will touch on a few simply strategies. Keeping in mind you may not be interested at all in developing property which is fine, this is just another form of income that you could potentially use and should be aware of.

The first is the most simple and the one that we have implemented the most often. We are not greedy and don't need to do the massive developments so, therefore, this has worked for us. It's the buy, bulldoze, build and hold strategy. The reason we bulldoze and build is that it adds value to the property immediately and then we get the capital growth on the higher improved value which speeds up the process to unlock some equity faster so that we can go out and buy the next investment property sooner. Again you want to make sure that you are purchasing in an area of good historical capital growth or a high socio economic area.

Renovating is another common tactic that a lot of people use.

By spending a little bit of money on a property you can increase its value making small profits as you go along. You can also find a property that isn't completed yet, e.g. something that a builder may have gone bust on. You can purchase it for a good price and fix it up yourself, then sell it and make significant profits as the person that was in control of the property just wants to get it sold! A half completed property is always a good find!

Other forms of development could be to subdivide a block of land and make one block of land into two. Again this is adding value to the block of land and you can sell half of it. This is something that is used a lot as people will sell one and pay off the other so they have as little debt as possible on the one that they keep. The other option is to construct on the second lot and then you can rent it out as another passive income stream, revalue the property, unlock some of the equity and use the unlocked equity/cash as a deposit on another investment property.

You can build a few townhouses, units or apartments on a block of land, subdividing the block and adding value to the block with the units which would be strata titled. If it were your intention to keep them all you may not strata title immediately. However, there are pros and cons for both as with strata titling all of the units you get that number of rates notices, however, you can also sell as many as you want when you want. Whereas if you do not strata title them you do not get multiple rates and in order to sell you would need to sell all of the units as 'one' lot. You could even build a whole apartment block if you wanted to; at the end of the day it is all about the numbers and funding and the desired outcome you are looking for.

Each strategy has different pros and cons and will all have a different result. The benefit to building one property on one block of land is that you don't have to go through as much hassle with council obtaining permits and neighbours possibly objecting. The time frame is a lot quicker and cost of it is a lot less. On the other hand, is there a high demand for big houses these days? Is the way of the future possibly splitting blocks into smaller ones and building smaller houses? If only we had a crystal ball! You need to weigh up what you are interested in and the returns you would get for each type of development that you do and make sure that you stick to your plan.

It is important to note that property development is an income stream to get you more money so that you can reinvest that money straight back into investment properties. Robert Kiyosaki in his book 'Rich Dad Poor Dad' says that he invests his money in stocks and the income he makes from this he puts straight into property. Again most of the people of the BRW richest 200 list either make or store their money in property.

Need assistance in deciding if property development is right for you so that you can 'work because you want to and not because you have to? Then get in touch with us and go to our website as we are here to help.

http://www.moneysecretsthatwork.com

CHAPTER 19
RISK MANAGEMENT

A lot of people don't invest money as they believe they will lose it and there is too high a risk of losing it or that it is simply too hard. Well if it were easy everyone would be doing it and then there would be no money in it! This chapter will look at some of the risks involved and how to manage them and make you feel a little bit more comfortable in investing and making money so that you can be financially free. At the end of the day property is bricks and mortar and will have value to it. Land cannot be made and can only go up in value with supply and demand and with the rising population there will always be demand.

Some of the common risks include:

INEXPERIENCE

By far the highest risk is inexperience (lack of knowledge). However, the good news is that help at the highest level, via education and mentoring is available. With that as a platform the other risks are readily containable. As I see it one of the flaws in our education system is that we are not allowed to copy off anyone else in our tests at school as they call it cheating, whereas in the real world all you need to do is to copy what other successful people do to become successful yourself. This is called modelling and it is easy to find people that will help you and show you the way to financial freedom and success so that you can work because you want to not because you have to. There are no new ideas in this book, just ideas that have stood the test of time - tried and tested methods to create wealth with proven results. My advice to you is to pick one strategy to start with (one that you like), go and learn it and follow it until you are successful at it.

People think that the costs are too high and would rather invest in shares. Shares are more risky than property because with property you are at least investing in bricks and mortar. Also with shares you have the potential to lose 100% of your money without the right education and strategies to protect your investment as share prices have been known to get down to zero. Do you remember Ansett, Onetell & Enron?

A lack of knowledge, lack of education and buying property based on emotion will greatly raise risk and may affect your ability to borrow.

I remember talking to my dad after a run that he went on where he was talking to a fellow runner about property. He was looking at buying an investment property and went to an auction where he believed the property was worth no more than $600,000. The property sold for $660,000. Dad asked his fellow runner who happened to be an old friend of his why he believed the property went for $660,000. His friend had no idea of the answer. He finally asked dad what the answer was, dad replied 'emotion.' Someone really wanted to live in that exact house and was willing to pay a premium for it because they really wanted it. As an investor we do not need to deal or bid against someone who is buying purely on emotion, we would love to sell our house to people on emotion, but no need to compete with them and to buy on emotion. On another occasion dad was driving down a street in Balwyn North and there was an auction going on and it appeared that the auction had stalled and no one was bidding and the bid price was well below what dad knew, from his research and due diligence of the area, what the property was worth. With one bid and lots of negotiation from the real estate agent dad finally bought it for $1,000 more than his original bid price and nearly $100,000 under its true value. So how do we know what its true value was? Well, everyone at the auction was looking at buying a house, a really nice house that in its day was in beautiful condition, but it was tired and needed some TLC. People fell in love with the house but did not want to do the work on it to bring it back to its former glory. Without emotion, and with knowledge and experience dad saw a block of land, bulldozed the house and sold the vacant land for nearly $100,000 profit. Dad was happy and the new owner was happy as he built a new house on the block which was worth approximately $100,000 more then he paid for it when it was completed and $400,000 within a couple of years.

People often like to be right; they would rather be right than rich. Ask yourself, what would you rather be, right or rich? If you don't know something, don't pretend like you do or don't think you do. Sometimes a little bit of knowledge is dangerous. It's only after you've received education and communicated with an expert that you realise how little you knew when you started.

On page 90 of Think of Grow Rich, Henry Ford is being questioned in court and was being asked general knowledge questions. After extensive questioning, Henry Ford became sick of answering them and said:

"Let me remind you that I have a row of electric push buttons on my desk and by pushing the right button I can summon to my aid men who can answer any question I desire to ask concerning the business which I am devoting most of my efforts. Now, will you kindly tell me why I should clutter up my mind with general knowledge for the purpose of being able to answer any question when I have men around me who can supply any knowledge I require."

So the moral of that story is you don't know what you don't know, and if you don't know something ask someone who can give you the information!

INTEREST RATE RISKS

The interest rate on borrowed funds could rise during the development or long term holding of the investment causing increased development and holding costs.

However, this is not world shattering. Let's say rates go up 1.5% gradually during a 12 month, four townhouse project. The actual increase in interest would be $1,500 per unit. Of course rates can also go down creating more profit. Also, when you apply for a loan with the bank, the bank will assess your borrowing capacity based on an interest rate normally 2% above the prevailing interest rate at the time. They do this in order to give themselves a buffer should interest rates rise and thereby reducing their risks when lending you money as well and making sure that a 2% interest rate, under similar circumstances, would not cause any undue financial hardship. The other opportunity you have to reduce Interest rate risk is to lock your interest rate in on a fixed rate for a specified period of time, for example 2, 3, 5 or 10 years. In order to do this you will need to be certain that you are holding the property for at least as long as the fixed term is; as it can be very expensive to terminate a fixed interest rate loan should interest rates go down.

MARKET RISKS

Property values can fall as well as rise. There is no guarantee as to the market value of your investment on completion, or, the demand for your investment should you desire to sell it.

Small, quick turnaround projects give market turnarounds less time to bite. Of course property values rise more often than they go down, so, over a longer period of time you will be in front, particularly if you are holding at least some of your product. Again this is more applicable for developing. Should you decide that this is not your preferred method (i.e. you are holding investment property for the long term, therefore, a quick turnaround) change in the market shouldn't affect your financial position. On an average project, values would need to drop by 15% before you would lose your first dollar.

This is also another reason why you should invest in positively cash flowed properties whereby you are not affected as much with rise or falls in the value of properties as week in and week out you are making money. If this is not possible, then you should try to invest in areas with proven capital growth history and minimise the negative cash flow as much as possible; or at least offset the negative cash flow with some positive cash flow properties for balance.

CONSTRUCTION RISKS

Costs can increase during construction because of disputes or unexpected delays caused by labour or material shortages, thereby lengthening the construction period resulting in increased holding charges.

Performing due diligence on the builder and using a lump sum fixed price and time contract can help minimise problems. You should also have some form of contingency in place when doing your own serviceability and financial analysis of the particular project or property. This contingency is there in case anything goes wrong. If everything goes according to schedule then you gain extra profit and returns from the project. If not, then you have accounted for this anyway, so it is not a surprise.

APPROVAL RISKS

Approval risks such as council town planning or state government approval are not valid for all Construction projects. However, they are applicable for such projects if you want to subdivide a block of land into multiple blocks, put more than one dwelling on a block, build apartments or townhouses or change the use of the land for which it currently has approval. The planning process can be as short as three months but can be as long as a number of years.

The obtaining of satisfactory planning and development approvals can be subject to time delays and unexpected costs. Neighbours may object to your plans, councils could be slow or reluctant to approve an application. Extra consultants might be required to supply special reports and infrastructure charges might increase.

Buying Development Approval approved sites, subject to existing Development Approval contracts and good pre-purchase due diligence can help minimise this risk as well as significantly reduce time frames. My advice is to ensure that you use expert consultants for planning advice and any planning approval applications so as to further minimise your risk as it is a specialist field.

FINANCIAL RISKS

Undercapitalisation means not having spare capital as a buffer if costs escalate. This is the biggest cause of a project to fail. As already mentioned building costs can increase and also holding costs especially if the construction is not finished on time due to planning or construction delays or even bad weather. The best thing to do for this is have a contingency buffer, this is also very important if you are renovating an investment property that is a little bit older, due to the unexpected surprises. The older the property is the more issues you could potentially have with it.

Another area that new investors in particular can get themselves into trouble is, 'over gearing.' By this I mean they borrow more than they are physically comfortable with borrowing, usually because they fall in love with a particular property and borrow too much. Over gearing is a massive issue for some people. A simple solution is a pre finance qualification to make sure that you are not getting stretched so far that it will put you in a position of financial hardship. The banks do this anyway before lending the money and again if you don't feel comfortable with the amount that you are borrowing simply reduce it until you do, so instead of borrowing 90-95% of the purchase value you borrow less, what you are comfortable with, maybe 80%. This still enables you to get into property and invest. Whilst you may not make as much money as you could if you were to leverage higher, you are still in and investing and the rental returns are also higher with the more cash you put in as mortgage repayments are less.

Need assistance with managing risk, or think it's too hard and just want to buy positive cash flowed investment properties so that you can 'work because you want to and not because you have to?' Then log on and register to our website as we are here to help.

http://www.moneysecretsthatwork.com

CHAPTER 20
CONTRACT TYPES AND STAMP DUTY

When saving for a property and buying a property a lot of people forget to take into account the extra costs such as stamp duty. There are also different contract types that can affect the amount of stamp duty and the costs of purchasing a property.

Three different contract types are:

1. Off the plan
2. Land and construct
3. Completed

Stamp Duty

This is an important topic to cover and can be crucial in deciding which type of contract you want to purchase. It could also be the difference between what contract type you can actually afford.

Stamp duty is a general tax imposed upon certain documents and some undocumented acquisitions; these include title transfers as a result of selling real estate, vehicles, business assets and other property, gifts, insurance policies and home loans, and is paid by the purchaser or borrower. In summary, it is an additional cash expense that you have to pay on top of the purchase price.

The amount of stamp duty that you have to pay varies from state to state.

Examples of Stamp Duty Calculations

On a property purchase with a dutiable value of $350,000, stamp duty will add to the overall costs:

$10,075 (Queensland)

$11,240 (NSW)

$12,250 (ACT)

$11,550 (Tasmania)

$9,800 (NT)

$10,735 (WA)

$13,830 (SA)

$13,870 (Victoria)

For a more expensive purchase, around $700,000 dutiable value, stamp duty will be between $24,525 (Queensland) and $37,070 (Victoria).

So you can see that stamp duty can add significant costs to purchasing property as once you have paid the deposit, you still need to find this additional money to complete the property purchase.

Off the Plan

For those of you who don't know what this is, it is when you purchase a property before the property is completed, generally before construction even begins, therefore, you are purchasing a property from just looking at the plans. There are both positives and negatives to purchasing off the plan; it would just depend on your personal situation.

One of the advantages of buying off the plan is that you will pay the current market price for a property, even though it will be completed in the future. For example, let's say you purchase a property which on today's market is valued at

$300,000. But as the property hasn't started construction yet, it might not be scheduled to finish for another 12 months or two years. Property prices have the potential to rise significantly during this period so you could have already got your money back before your property has even finished being built.

You are able to secure a high value asset for a low initial capital outlay. What this means is to purchase a property you will only need a deposit and then you pay the balance upon completion and settlement of the property. While a deposit is made to secure the property (usually 10%), the entire payment doesn't need to be paid until the property has been built. This provides you with time to organise your finances and if required sell your existing home without the need for bridging finance.

You may be able to have significant stamp duty savings in some states. State governments (in certain states) offer bonuses and reductions in stamp duty for buying off the plan, which in turn can save you thousands of dollars. For example in Queensland you have to pay stamp duty on the full amount, whereas, in Victoria you pay it on the property value of 'the date of the contract' which can be significantly lower compared to the completed property value. As the property is not built yet you are solely paying stamp duty on the land component. Let's have a look at the example we spoke about earlier. You purchase a property in Victoria for $300,000 with a land component of $80,000. If you buy this off the plan then you pay stamp duty on the $80,000 which is $2,100 as opposed to the full $300,000 which is $14,041.

Land and Construct

Again, there are pros and cons to this type of contract.

How this works is that your property is split into two contracts. The first being land: So you purchase the land and then settle on that. The positive to this is that you pay stamp duty on the land component which is just the land price rather than the completed property price so there are large stamp duty savings to be made as demonstrated by the above example for an 'off the plan' purchase.

Once you have settled on the land you then construct the property, whereby you make pay progress payments to the builder. The negative to this is that you pay interest during the building process and you won't have any tenants in their paying rent. You need to weigh up the costs and whether or not you believe that this contract type will benefit you as on one hand you have significantly lower stamp duty prices, on the other hand you won't have tenants in them yet but you are still required to pay interest during construction.

It solely depends on your situation as normally progress payments are still significantly less than the full stamp duty amount. You also don't have to find the full stamp duty amount straight away as it could take a while to save for that amount. Progress payments are like a payment plan and you only have to pay small amounts at a time. Again you have the potential for your property to go up in value before the final completion time of the property.

Completed Property

This contract type is pretty self-explanatory. The property is completed, there is one contract and the tenants can already be in there or move in straight away. You can negotiate the terms of your contract for price and settlement periods. Stamp duty will be high and will be based on the contract price.

Need assistance with finding a property that would best suit your scenario and so you can 'work because you want to and not because you have to.' Then register to our website as we are here to help you.

http://www.moneysecretsthatwork.com

CHAPTER 21
FINANCE

Over the years I have learnt that finance is the most important aspect about property. Why you may ask? This is because of the term I used before called 'leverage.' In order to become wealthy you need to use others people money, so in order to do this you must obtain finance from somewhere, most people use the banks for this. As a result you need to understand how you can obtain finance and get the best possible deal for finance so that you are in the best position to save money, leverage money and get the best value for your money!

The first question you need to ask yourself is, 'do you use a finance broker or do you go to a bank?' If you are thinking about going directly to a bank without using a finance broker just think about this example. If you went into a BMW dealer, do you think they are going to sell you a Mercedes Benz, a Porsche or a Lexus, or are they going to sell you a BMW? This is the same when you go into a major bank or a lending institution. If you go into Westpac Bank they are going to try to sell you their products and tell you about what they have to offer and not what is best for you. They are not going to sell you a CBA loan or an NAB loan; they will simply sell you their product. This doesn't really give you the greatest range of loans or give you an understanding of what is out there in the market place.

If you want to build a house, do you do it yourself or employ a professional to do it for you? If you are sick, do you diagnose yourself or do you go and see a doctor? If you want to invest in property do you go and ask your mate that is broke and never owned a property in his life or do you speak with a successful property investor? The point is depending on what you want, and what you want to do, then you go and see a professional in that field to make sure that you're doing it properly. Even the most elite sportspeople in the world all have coaches. This just shows the power of mentoring and also employing professionals to make sure you are in the best position for you. With this is mind it is best that when you do finance that you use a professional as they have the knowledge and are employed to do the best thing for you and not another BMW salesmen trying to sell you a BMW. If the finance broker doesn't get you a loan or a good deal and you are not happy with them, they won't make any money and you won't go back to them. It is in their best interest to do the best job they can for you. I am not saying that in some instances it is not good to go straight to a bank but make sure you have looked at all your options and at least understand what you are doing and why you are going directly to a bank. Don't just go to that particular bank as you have an account set up with them and are loyal to them as they might not have the best loan for you.

I personally have a Certificate IV in Finance (Mortgage Broking) and also a Diploma of Finance. These are the two qualifications that are required to be a qualified mortgage consultant or broker, whichever one you want to call it. Knowing the finance industry gives you a better chance of getting money, also what is happening in the market and also giving you the best deal providing you with the most money. It also puts me in a better position to help the clients I am dealing with. It is much better for me to be able to know straight away what kind of properties we can look at and what sort of plan we need to put in place to make sure my clients can get into the properties they want. With lending rules changing all the time it is important to stay ahead of the game. When you are using other people's money you want to know how to get the most of it with the best terms!

So why are most Australian's, despite living in a rich country, not rich themselves? Because at school they are not taught how to become investors, despite the fact that every single Australian needs to become a millionaire in their lifetime in order to retire comfortably.

(The latest superannuation industry stats say you need $1.1 - $1.3M for a comfortable retirement)

So when people think finance they think financial planner. Why? Because the Government advises Australians to go and visit a licence financial planner before they do any form of investing. Which is not intelligent nor is it common sense. Yet so many Australians have them and listen to them each and every single day.

I ask you again: If you want to be rich, who should you study?

A) A rich person

B) A poor person

It's obvious you don't need a financial planner. Australians need their own Financial Education.

Do you know how much investing financial planners have to do before they can get a license?

Zero.

Nil.

None.

Would you take your car to a mechanic who'd never had any experience fixing cars?

Would you allow a doctor, who'd never operated on someone before, to operate on you?

Would you even go to a hairdresser who'd only done a 2-week course from a manual and never actually cut hair before?

Would you fly in a plane with a pilot who had never flown before?

Of course you wouldn't.

Why then would you to go see a financial planner, who in most cases has never invested at all? And one, who has certainly not invested into the high commission paying, managed fund they're trained to sell you.

Finance is not about financial planning, it is about using others people's money and leverage. Many people are not clear about how to get a loan, what loan they qualify for and what kind of applicant they are. That again is why it is good to know and why you go and see an expert in the field. Even if you walk into a branch one person in the branch might tell you one thing and another person might tell you another. There is even conflict in the branch as they are sometimes not 100% aware of their own policies and products.

There are two types of applicants when applying for loans, one is a Full Doc loan applicant and the other is a Lo Doc loan applicant. Now there is a pretty distinct difference between the two of them. If you work for someone else and you receive a pay slip from them, they put the money straight into your bank account and take the tax out on a periodic basis; you are normally a full doc applicant. If you are self-employed you are generally a Lo doc applicant, however, this is not in every case. If you are self-employed but can provide both business and personal tax returns for the past 2 years, then you can still be classified as a Full Doc applicant.

You might be wondering why any of this is important and why does it matter what type of applicant I am. Well banks will lend a maximum of 80% to Lo doc applicants as they consider them to be in the higher risk category. This can be a big difference considering full doc applicants can borrow up to 95%. The other major difference is that there is also a thing in finance called Lenders Mortgage Insurance (LMI). This is applicable for full doc clients above 80% whereas for Lo doc clients it is applicable above 60%. Now again, you might think, 'why is this important?' Well, LMI can be very expensive and cost you a lot of money.

A point of distinction between the two types of borrowing types is Lender's Mortgage Insurance.

I just want to give you an example of how expensive LMI is but also explain how it could work to your benefit to borrow more money. Let's use a $500,000 purchase price as an example as it's a little bit lower than Melbourne's medium house price. If you were to have a loan at 95% then LMI would cost you about $15,000. Well just short of it, depending on which LMI company you have to go with. Banks will only accept a certain LMI funder. Some banks have their own LMI and their own calculations, but a good ball park figure would be around $15,000.

So how do you decide to use LMI or not? This is a personal preference and again it can be used to your advantage. Some banks allow you to borrow the LMI so you just pay Interest Only over a 30 year period which makes it pretty cost effective. However, banks will cap the Loan to Value Ratio (the maximum amount of money you can borrow compared to the purchase price or valuation); whichever is the lower, to 97%. This all sounds too hard? So you get a loan without LMI which would have an LVR of 80%. This would give you borrowings of $400,000 which means you have to put in an extra $100,000 of your own money. Alternatively, you decide to go up to 95% and bear the costs of paying LMI. This gives you an additional $75,000 of borrowings as you can now borrow $475,000. So you can now pay $15,000 and get $75,000 which makes you $60,000 better off. However, some banks will even allow you to just add the LMI to your loan so you do not actually have to come up with any of the $15,000 at all; you just pay the interest on the higher amount.

So why would you do this in the real world? Let's say you had the borrowing capacity, the serviceability and the $100,000 deposit with an 80% LVR you could buy one $500,000 property. Or alternatively with a 95% LVR you could buy four $500,000 properties. If they are all positive cash flow you are making four times the amount of money each week and now you have capital growth on $2,000,000 worth of property which at say 6% per annum is $120,000 instead of capital growth on one property worth $500,000 which at 6% per annum is $30,000. Don't you love the power of leverage?

So now that we have covered LMI; - how it can be beneficial and how it might be important to be a full doc applicant. At the time of writing this book there is also another downside to being self-employed. Currently most if not all banks have a requirement that before you can get a loan you need to have an Australian Business Number (ABN) for a minimum period of 2 years. If you intend on being self-employed at some point in your life you might as well get an ABN set up so that way your two years can start from now as opposed to having to wait another 2 years down the track before you can get a loan.

CREDIT SCORING

Credit scoring is something new to Australia and something that everyone needs to be aware of when applying for a loan. Banks use credit scoring these days and do credit tests and most clients do not know that they do this or know that it can affect their loan application. It could be the difference between getting approval for a loan and not getting approval for a loan. The banks don't tell you what they put on the credit tests but we have an idea of all the things that contribute.

This can be vital to obtaining a loan and a lot of people fail on credit scoring even though they pass the other tests. There are little things that you can do to help pass this test as you get points for some things and you lose points for other things. I will discuss a few of them now and give you just a few handy hints that might help you along the way so that you might avoid failing a credit score.

CREDIT CARDS

Credit cards are the first thing I will touch on as I believe it is the most important. Little do people realise the impact of a credit card, or two for that matter. Credit cards can be the difference between obtaining a loan and not obtaining a loan.

Obviously everyone knows that credit cards are seen as a bad thing if you are in debt and constantly in debt on them. They can also be very bad if you have high limits on them. Most of you will have experienced the bank offering you higher limits on your credit cards and you might jump at the opportunity as they are handing you more money. Next time they do you might want to rethink accepting after you finish reading the impact credit cards and high limits have on your loan application. Having said that a credit card with a low limit, paid off monthly can be a very good thing and actually help towards credit scoring.

As I mentioned, when conducting a credit scoring test the banks will give you points; we can call them green flags, and take away points, we can call these red flags. The longer you have a credit card with good credit history means the more 'bonus' points you get, this can be seen as a green flag. However, if you constantly owed money on your credit card and didn't pay it off to zero every month, this would be a red flag. I suggest having one credit card with a low limit, and make sure you pay it off every month.

Now, what happens if you don't pay it off? As soon as you don't pay it off you start paying interest, and the interest rate is generally very high. Despite the fact that you have that high interest rate until you pay it off, many people keep using their credit card, increasing the amount of interest that they are paying. Let's just use an example and say that you have to pay an interest amount of $50 a month because you were lazy, didn't follow the rules and didn't pay your credit card off. This is $600 a year in interest that you have to pay to the bank. How much better would that be in your pocket? You still have to pay the bank what you owe them; this is an additional $600 out of your pocket. Could you not have better spent that money on other things? That can effectively be a gym membership for a whole year. If you keep throwing away $600 a year every time you decide to be lazy this adds up to a lot of money. In summary, the longer you have a credit card with good credit rating the better it is and also the more money you will save!

Another general misconception about credit cards is the amount that it actually costs you when you apply for a loan. If you have a limit of $10,000 but pay your credit card to $0 every month, some people think that their credit card doesn't count; so they don't tell the finance broker about it when going through their assets and liabilities for a loan submission. This is a very dangerous game because the bank can find you out about this and then we are in trouble. But just to explain the impact of a high credit card limit, the rule of thumb is that a credit cards eats up 6 times the borrowing capacity, so that would cost you roughly $60,000 in borrowing capacity! That is a lot of money if you are looking at borrowing money to purchase a $300,000 investment property. That's a lot of money full stop, nearly the average Australian wage just because you have a credit card limit of $10,000. If you were to simply reduce the credit card limit to what you need to live off for the month then this would be substantially more beneficial than having a $10,000 limit on your credit card. That is living a very lucrative lifestyle. Having a $3,000 limit might be more appropriate as it will only reduce your borrowing capacity by $18,000 when applying for a housing or investment loan. This is significantly different from the $60,000 that it was eating up of your borrowing capacity. Another little trick I have seen people use is to reduce their credit card limit to as little as possible whilst applying for the loan, then once they have submitted the loan and been approved they raise the limit again.

OTHER HELPFUL TIPS

Even if you are young reading this book and think you are not old enough for any of this to affect you, you have the ability to help your credit score from a young age. Putting your phone in your own name as opposed to it being in your parents name and conducting your phone bill properly will help your credit score. But if the phone is already in your name and you miss a few payments this affects your credit score and you are marked with red flags. A lot of people start going to the gym at the age of 16, paying this in your name could also help you get points, but again missing payments is not ideal.

Also when paying credit cards, how often do people pay off their credit cards in whole numbers? As in, if you owe $48.75 you simply just pay $50 off it. Why this may sound very miniscule it does make a difference. If you pay your credit cards off in whole numbers you might think that it is a good thing as you're paying more, the bank think differently and mark it as a red flag as they think that you have been in debt with the bank and have entered into a debt repayment agreement with them. As I touched on a little bit earlier, living off your credit card for the month then paying it back to zero can be very beneficial. You can look at putting all your income into an offset account and use your credit card to live off and swipe it back to zero every month. This is helpful as you should not spend tomorrow's money today; you need to make sure you control it and that you are not spending more than what you should be and never put yourself in a position where you are always playing 'catch up.'

Another thing that people are not aware of is your Credit Reporting Agency (CRA report). Each time you do something that requires the lending of money you receive a hit on your CRA. I had a lady that went into 7 different car dealerships and each one of them put 'a hit' on her CRA. She then found out when she applied for her loan that 7 different hits on her CRA is a bad thing, even if it simply for a car. Once you receive a hit on your CRA it doesn't just go away after a week, it is there for 5 years! The more hits you have on your CRA, the higher risk you are and again the less likely a bank will be to take you on for finance. They think, 'well if none of these people have taken you on I'm not going to take you on either' as they see you as high risk. If car dealerships won't take her on for a $30,000 loan, why would a bank take her on for a $300,000 property loan? Be aware of this as this is crucial when going for a loan. I've had so many people ask me, 'why can't we just submit the loan to all the lenders at the same time?' You can't simply just put your application into all the banks and hope one of them gives it to you. None of them will approve your loan due to all your hits on the CRA. So you need to be careful with how many times you do things, and apply for things, as they all contribute to credit scoring and your credit rating.

Other smaller things that you might not be able to control as much include things like; how many times you have moved house. Whilst it may be a bit out of your control some lenders don't care and might rate this as pretty bad. If you have a home phone number you get points, a mobile, a fax number, an email address or work number. The more information they have about you the more points that you get.

Again more things that are out of your control might be how many years you have been working for the same company, working in the same position, the same industry. The banks are after consistency, and the longer you do something or remain in the same place, the higher they rate you and the lower risk they will put on you.

In summary my advice is to reduce the number of credit cards that you hold and the limit on your credit cards, pay them off back to zero on a monthly basis and ensure all of your bills are paid in full and on time. In other words, do whatever it takes to protect your credit rating as a bad rating not only affects you today but for years to come.

Need assistance with finance so that you can be in the position to 'work because you want to and not because you have to?' Then visit and register to our website as we are happy to help.

http://www.moneysecretsthatwork.com

100% Offset Account

If you are new to investing you may not have heard of 100% offset accounts but they are something that you can apply for when getting a loan. It is very simple and I believe they are a very good thing if you can get a loan that has this facility. Not all loans have this facility, however, if you are disciplined with your spending they can save you thousands and thousands over the life time of your loan if used correctly and, therefore, should be considered if available with your loan.

They have significant benefits; the main one is to reduce interest repayments. A redraw account works similar; however, you get more tax benefit out of a 100% offset account.

Let's look at how a 100% offset account works. I suggest with all loans for people to pay Interest Only repayments as you get the choice to pay off more of your loan if you so wish to. For example, if you have a loan worth $300,000 at an interest rate of 6.5% and pay Interest Only on a monthly basis and it has a 100% offset attached to this account. Currently there is no money in the offset account so each month you pay Interest Only on $300,000. You then say, but I want to now start paying some money off my loan. So you want to pay $10,000 off your loan, instead of putting this into the loan account and never seeing it again, you put it into your 100% offset account. Your monthly interest repayments will now be on $290,000. If you put another $90,000 in there then your interest repayments will only be on $200,000.

Another benefit to the 100% offset account is that you can take the money out again whenever you want to. Banks these days very rarely give out Line of Credits (LOC). So a 100%

offset accounts effectively works like a LOC as you can take the money out whenever you want to and use it for whatever purpose you want without the bank asking anything about it. If you were to pay this directly off the loan amount that you owe the bank you would never see that money again. The 100% offset account gives you flexibility and options. An example if you then decided to take that $100,000 out of the 100% offset account you would be paying interest repayments on $300,000 again. Why is this more effective than just putting the extra money into another bank account I hear you ask? If you put it into another bank account the interest rate would be significantly lower say 4% and you would be required to pay tax on any interest received.

Sometimes banks charge a fee to have this account, so it might not be worth it depending on the loan size and how much money you are likely to be actually putting into the account. A redraw facility effectively does the same thing, but the banks won't charge you to have this account. If you are not sure what is best speak to your finance broker or accountant as they should be able to help you out with making the decision.

FINANCE CONTINUED

Being good at finance and having the right finance broker for you can make a massive difference in the overall wealth and value of your account. It can also make a big difference if you are like Robert Kiyosaki and not overly concerned about your net worth and more interested in your monthly passive income.

It is therefore, vitally important that you choose your broker carefully and use a reputable broker. The industry is becoming more regulated as I write this book; however, in the past some finance brokers may not have had the best interests of their clients at heart and some do things for commission rather than finding the best possible deal for the client. I personally believe in the long term value of a client and doing everything I can to help them and I try and make sure I set them on the road to financial freedom. As I already mentioned, getting the right finance is crucial. Using someone else's money is the key to your success and leverage. If you cannot get access to someone else's money then it is a lot harder to become rich as you have to make it all yourself.

Some people think that they don't need a finance broker and can go straight to the branch. If using a finance broker won't cost you any more money, or worst case scenario will cost you a few dollars, however, they have a better chance of getting you the best possible loan, why wouldn't you do it? If you go to the bank and get it wrong because you missed something or didn't know something, then this has an effect on your CRA and could impact on any future deals that you may do. It is not worth the risk. Make sure that you do everything in your power to get the loan across the line first time.

I can't emphasise enough the power of leverage and using other people's money. I have shown the difference between Interest Only and Principal and Interest, however, it is also important to be aware that there can be a big difference in the interest rate that you receive. This is more critical on the loan size as the dollar savings that you will receive for having a low interest rate with a small loan amount is a lot less than having a low interest rate with a high loan amount. There are more savings to be made at the higher end so if you have a smaller loan the interest rate might not be as important. At the end of the day it is not just the interest rate or the term of the loan or whether it is Interest Only or Principal and Interest, or whether it has 100% offset, it is a combination of all of the above. It is the entire deal that is important.

For example:

$250,000 at 6.5% is $16,250 per year.

$250,000 at 7% is $17,500 per year.

That's a difference of $1,250 per year.

But the higher the loan amount the more impact interest rates could have on your bottom line.

$1,000,000 at 6.5% is $65,000

$1,000,000 at 7% is $70,000

That is $5,000 difference per year and a lot bigger difference than the lower amount.

So on face value the 6.5% interest rate is the deal that looks the best, however, if this bank is only offering you 80% of the purchase price or $800,000 on a $1,000,000 purchase; whereas the bank at 7% is offering you 95% of the purchase price that is a difference of $150,000. Now which deal is better? I would argue that it would be worth paying the extra $5,000 per year in higher interest in order to free up the additional $145,000 of cash that you could use to buy another positive cash flow investment property.

Quiz:

Do you have more than one credit card?

Are your limits higher than what they need to be?

Do you have a finance broker?

Do you use enough of other people's money in your investing?

Do you think not using LMI's saves you money?

Need assistance with finance and using other people's money so that you can 'work because you want to and not because you have to?' Then visit our website and register as we are here to help.

http://www.moneysecretsthatwork.com

CHAPTER 22
DIFFERENCE BETWEEN SAVING AND INVESTING

As I mentioned at the start there are two different types of people. There are spenders and then there are savers. Then there is also spending and investing. There is also saving and investing. So this chapter will aim to distinguish the difference between them and look at how it is in your interests to invest in property rather than just leaving your money in an interest bearing bank account. An interest bearing bank account is one of those bank accounts that earns you anywhere between 0.1% and maybe 6% if you are really lucky and interest rates go up.

The essential difference between saving and investing is that saving is primarily a result of restraining from spending, and you put that spare cash into the bank. Investing on the other hand is the utilisation of accumulated funds through leverage to purchase wealth creation vehicles such as assets that provide income, capital growth or both. There is a saying that I love by Robert Kiyosaki, 'you rent your lifestyle and buy income producing assets.'

So there are three types of savings, short term, medium term and long term. The short term savings is when you just have your money in a bank account and you earn the interest that the bank gives you. You have easy access to this and you can put money in and take money out whenever you want.

Medium term is when you put money in a 'term deposit.' This is when you give money to the bank for a designated period of time. This means that you cannot touch it during that time, however, as a trade off the bank will give you a higher interest rate. Other fixed interest items are bonds, debentures, certificates of deposit, promissory notes. I would consider this to be anywhere from 3 months to ten years.

Long term savings is when you save for retirement and your money is in a superannuation account typically this could be from when you commence paid employment until retirement at age 65 or older, somewhere in the vicinity of 45 – 50 years.

So with these types of investing, most people would have some form of short term savings account. Less people would have medium and even less would have any idea about their long term savings accounts. As most of you would have short term savings accounts, how many of you actually look at your accounts, and compare banks and compare their interest rates? Whilst the interest rate difference maybe small the end difference may be quite large over a long period of time. If all it takes is to monitor this and to change banks if necessary and put your money in different accounts to earn you more, why wouldn't you do it? This is a very easy wealth creating mechanism and it's generating you money you otherwise wouldn't have and a result of the power of compounding (which is earning interest on interest when the interest that you receive is re invested back into the investment). One problem with this strategy is that it can take a long period of time.

INFLATION

My mother had the opinion for a while to just put all her money into a bank account and just live of this. This is a good idea and can work but, you can make so much more by doing other things with your money. In reality you are not getting very good returns as your money is not leveraged in the bank. As I already mentioned, how hard would it have been for Mike Tyson to spend all his money, the $400 million, considering the amount he would have been receiving if he just had his money in the bank earning interest at let's say at 5% that would have been $20 million per year.

Inflation is a massive part of why interest from the bank isn't the best investment strategy. As discussed earlier it is still good and you should look at doing this for your money in order to get you started but I will show you the effect of inflation on your savings and income and why you have to become an investor and use leverage as soon as possible.

So let's say that you have your money invested in the bank at 6%. You think, that's a pretty good return I might not have to put my money into my loan account, I'm nearly getting higher than the interest on loans! What you forget is that you lose 3.1% of it straight away to inflation! This is a lot of the 6% that you thought you were getting. Then you have to pay tax of let's say 32% (which is low). After that you are now left with your actual income that you make. So 6% minus tax of 1/3 which is 4% then you lose inflation which is 3.1% so you are now down to 0.9% of your money. But if you invest this in bricks and mortar and leverage your money, what are your returns there? Will they still be 0.9%? What if inflation for that year was a little bit higher than 3.1%?

Let's now say you invested your money into property as opposed to just letting your money sit in a bank account. So you purchased a $300,000 property using a 90% LVR so you have invested $30,000 of your own money. So, in the next year inflation is 3.1%. What does this mean? Well, when inflation goes up, what happens to the rents? They also go up. What happens to property prices over time? They go up in value at an average of 9% per annum. So our rent and capital growth cover the inflation and we are making returns on $300,000 as opposed to our $30,000 so our money is leveraged 10 times more.

These are things we need to consider and why property investing can make you lots of money and mean that you can work because you want to and not because you have to!

Quiz:

Do you have any savings systems?

Are you investing your money instead of saving?

Do you have any systems for investing?

Need assistance with better utilising your money so that you can 'work because you want to and not because you have to?' Then register to our website as we are here to help.

http://www.moneysecretsthatwork.com

CHAPTER 23
MULTIPLE STREAMS OF INCOME

Almost all the gurus talk about multiple streams of income and how you should have passive income. I particularly like T Harv Eker's theory as he puts multiple streams of income into perspective.

You can't be a master at everything; you need to learn things one at a time. How many years or training sessions does it take you to be good at something, let alone master it? Professional sports people train and play their whole lives to be good at what they do. Many people try to take on more than one strategy at a time and as a result they are distracted from their main goal. As a result they master nothing and, therefore, never achieve financial success and freedom.

It is good, therefore, to have multiple streams of income, but remember not to do it all at once; you need to do one at a time. Start with one, master that then move onto the next one. Systemise, monetise, residualise, multiply, automate the first process and then move onto your second stream of income and do the same all over again.

The benefit to having multiple streams of income is that you are diversified, so that if something bad happens to one section of your income or your portfolio you are covered by having other forms of income to protect you. You also want to have more passive income so that you have more choices in life to do the things you want to do. The ultimate objective here is to have enough passive income coming in to replace your existing income (JOB) and to pay for your desired lifestyle, whatever that maybe.

You might be thinking, 'how do I access capital growth income?' Well, there are two ways and yes one is selling the property in which case you will need to pay a little capital Gains Tax and you lose the future growth and cash flow from that property, but, it may be a strategy that you employ in order to reduce debt. It may even turn out that one of your properties is not performing as well as it should and therefore you decide to get rid of the property that is the worst performer in your portfolio. The other and probably easiest and best thing to do is simply just refinance your property. What I mean here is as the value of the property goes up in value, you go back to the bank and have the property revalued and you borrow more money against the new valuation. This strategy works very well in a rising market but you must also be aware that when you borrow more against a property that also means the amount of interest you are paying to the bank also goes up and needs to be taken into account in your cash flows and planning strategy. This strategy may not work in a falling market or where bank lending criteria is tight as this is where they become very wary about who they lend to and how much they lend. This was particularly true during and after the Global Financial Crisis (GFC) of 2008.

Land banking is another common strategy used by some people and can be extremely well suited to Self Managed Super Funds. Land Banking is where land is bought outside the urban growth boundary or in a different zone. Land is bought here in the hope that the government or council will change the zoning of this property; this will instantly increasing the value of the land or where a major developer, such as Stockland, Villawood, Peet or Central Equity has a tract of land ready to develop but are awaiting council approval.

In order to be really good at anything in life ideally you need to enjoy what you are doing and therefore you may need to try a couple of the different strategies until you find the one that is right for you. When you find your strategy stick with it, learn all about it and work it until it is systemised, monetised, automated, risdualised, and then repeat it again and again. This is no different to finding your second and subsequent income streams, find something that you are interested in. If you are interested in America and the ups and downs of that market where at the time of writing you can buy houses at 70 – 80 % discount compared to where they were at prior to the GFC you might want to look at investing in that. If you like Foreign Exchange then you can look at trading in currencies. If you like businesses you may wish to buy an existing business that you can build up and then later sell or turn it into your next passive income stream. If you are interested in food then you may wish to look at investing in commodities. The choices are almost limitless but of course the key to whatever you choose is to systemise, automate, residualise, monetise and duplicate.

With the different forms of income that you do decide to pursue, make sure you are dealing profitably though as the whole point of this is; multiple streams of income rather than multiple streams of expenditure. Again I would like to highlight; make sure you do one thing properly first before you move on to your next thing.

You might not have any interest in any of these other classes of assets and just love property, like my dad, well that is still

OK as you can diversify your risk by investing in different properties around Australia. You can have properties all in different cities as the property market in different cities and different states performs differently at different times. You may also diversify by investing in units, apartments, townhouses and houses. Whatever your strategy and plan is, follow that. You have to be comfortable with your plan.

FINANCIALLY FREE

What does Financially Free actually mean?

My definition is having enough passive income, that is income that you do not have to work for, such as rent, dividends, interest being paid to you, royalties, trailing commissions etc., so that it replaces your existing income and provides you with enough surplus cash to live whatever lifestyle you so choose to live.

Depending on how old you are, reading this book 'financially free' may mean something different to you. If you have been working for a very long time and you want to get out of the rat race, the day-to-day routine of going to work to earn an income at a job just in order to pay your bills so that you can survive for another week, you will probably do almost anything it takes to be financially free. Your goal will be to become financially free by starting to do the things in this book, like have a spending system, start getting some education and start investing in property. It will not be easy as you have old habits that need to be changed, however, the end result certainly makes getting started well worth the effort in the end. If you are younger it can also be difficult to break the existing cycle as you believe that your still young and your just here to have a good time and that you go to work to get money so that you can go out and have a good time and with the money left over hopefully support yourself. Being financially free is probably not as important and a lot of you would never have even heard the term financially free before let alone know what it is or want to achieve it. That being said, it only takes a very small change to become financially free if you are just starting out as you probably still live at home and in fact have very few expenses. The major change for you if you are young is to understand and comprehend the fact that if you do without a little today you can have anything you want in the future.

Whilst it might sound silly, having multiple streams of income at the start when you are young might not be required. I want people to understand the power of being young and beginning to invest early and being smart with your money. When you are young you are earning very little money and also have very little expenses. You might still be at university and working part time, or just graduated university and find yourself first year out working full time on a low wage. So if you are on a low wage and have very little expenses, how easy is it to replace your income by using and spending your money a little bit smarter? The key is to start the jar system right away; a minimum of 10% to the Financially Free Account, 10% to the Long Term Savings for Spending , 10% for your education, 5% for charity, 10% for the Fun Account, and 55% for the necessities, just by implementing this system alone you can become financially free and wealthy over time.

I want everyone to think how much better your life would be if you doubled your income! This is what financially free means; you replace your income so you have a choice to work. Then if your young and you choose to work, then you can and you have doubled your income! Then on the weekend you might have a BBQ on a chartered boat, just for fun! But again if making more money isn't important to you, and that is probably because you're currently broke, then continue to spend your money and do whatever you want with it and don't worry about becoming financially free.

Need assistance becoming financially free so that you can 'work because you want to and not because you have to?' Register to our website as we are here to help.

http://www.moneysecretsthatwork.com

CHAPTER 24
MINDSET

The best thing that you can do is to keep improving yourself. If you get your psychology mastered you will be successful in life! Your psychology doesn't just happen once; you can't do something once and be good at it forever. You need to keep practicing, that's why in sport you have to train and you also have a coach so that you don't lose the skill you have and to ensure that you continue improving. Even the best sportspeople in the world have to continuously train and they all have coaches. You may be familiar with the expression 'if you don't use it you lose it?' This is the same with psychology and constantly improving/bettering yourself. You always need to do something! Another saying is, 'if you are standing still you are actually going backwards.' What this means is that because of inflation, technology and advances in the world if you are not at least doing something to keep up you are in fact falling behind and therefore going backwards. Your position relative to everything around you is getting worse.

I would like to start with an example of how much money I have spent to improve myself, well just rough figures anyway just to give you an idea. If I didn't spend any money on improving myself I wouldn't have known half the things I do now and have learnt how to make money to write this book. I went to school, I attended a private school which is roughly $20,000 a year, however, I only spent 2 years there so that's a total of $40,000. I went to university for 4 years, that's $8,000 per year so another $32,000. I have attended lots of personal development courses; a 6 grand course, 3 grand course, 6 grand, 3 grand here and 3 grand there, it all adds up. Out of the courses I have done I did a property development seminar, now from this 3 day intensive bootcamp I learnt more than the four years I spent at university spending $32,000 doing a Property Degree.

So let's look at the model that most people are taught. Go to school, get a good education, go to university and get the best job you can. Let's look at how much money that would actually cost you.

So your mum and dad sent you to a private school for your high school years, that's 20 grand a year for 6 years, so $120,000 then you go to university because you had a good education and you spend another 4 years there that's another $32,000 grand. So now you're up to $152,000 that you have spent on your education to get a first year paying job of around $50,000. Is it all worth it or is there another way? It's a bit like the start of the book where I said surely we don't have to work 9-5 all the time. Going out and doing boot camps and courses from people with results rather than a certificate is certainly a start. You spend a lot less money than attending university and going to a private school and yes you actually get taught results rather than theory. So it's not just about how much money you spend it's what you get from the results that you spend.

Pat Mesiti is my personal favourite speaker. I have attended his seminars on numerous occasions and no matter how often he would repeat something or how many times I see him, he is fantastic each time and I always learn something new or pick up on a new distinction. The content that he talks about is amazing. Therefore, I have learnt a lot of my mindset stuff from him as he is someone that I learn well from. As I have already said, I think mindset is very important and the best thing that you can do is to keep improving yourself. If you get your psychology mastered you will be successful in life!

A lot of people do things out of emotions, especially when you are investing your money, emotions come into your calculations a lot. This is something we need to work on and you need to feel comfortable with investing your money so that you don't get stuck in this trap. A lot of this comes down to knowledge, and you do not know enough about the property market, or finance or investing in stocks, or options trading, or CFD's etc. If you don't know something, learn it or copy from someone who does know it. This is where mindset comes in. You have to have a reason to be rich and want to have a better life and need the mindset to admit that you don't know everything and maybe you can learn something from someone else or copy from someone else that is already successful and has done what you are trying to do. You also need to give yourself permission to be successful. You deserve to be rich!

Whilst I say Pay Mesiti is my favourite speaker it doesn't mean that he is the only person that you can learn from. There is a famous quote from Henry Ford 'whether you think you can, or you think you can't, you're right.' Now I think that this is very powerful. I personally know so many people out there that have the most negative minds and they don't see it and have no intention of changing it. I've never met anyone that has a negative mind and also has millions of dollars. The two just do not go together, they simply repel each other.

People that watch all the news programs each day, they are

key culprits to this. How often on the news is there anything happy or uplifting shown? I know they tried doing a happy news show once and no one watched it so they reverted back to the doom and gloom stuff just to get higher ratings. But just more bad and negative things happen on these news programs that end up programming your head. I say this all the time to people; it all depends on who and what you associate yourself with. If you go into a prison an innocent man, you are going to come out a criminal. If you are hanging around criminals all the time; you are going to learn a thing or two. If you hang around with Donald Trump all the time I'm sure you are going to learn a thing or two about making money. If you watch the news all the time that's negative, you are going to start thinking like that to. You want to try and associate yourself with the good things in life and think positively and make sure your head is right so that when an opportunity arises you can actually see it and take action. If you think you can do something, you can. If you keep telling yourself your rubbish at this and I can't do it, guess what, you will be rubbish at it and you won't be able to do it. Changing your life starts with changing your mind! Whether you think you can, or you think you can't, you're right!

I can't tell you how many people have told me or posted on Facebook the term FML. Now I can't say what the first letter stands for but the second two stand for 'my life' and the first word is a naughty word so I'm sure you can put two and two together. Now in my opinion the people that say this are either frustrated with everything going on around them, or attention seekers as they have very good lives. They just don't appreciate the things they have and respect the things they have. We often take things for granted. How many times have you heard the expression 'you don't appreciate what you have until it's gone.' Well in these cases these people don't appreciate what they have. My friend Rohan James just wrote a book about this as well called 'The Yoga Revolution.' This is all about trying to get people to understand the messed up world that we live in and appreciate the things and people we have in our life. Well, this is the interpretation that I got out of it anyway. In my opinion this is very important as we need to be comfortable with ourselves and appreciate the things we have in order to move forward. This is why goal setting and planning is so important and finding out what we want out of life and also what your partner wants out of life, as you can't do something without his or her acceptance or permission.

One of my favourite quotes from Pat is 'what is easy to do is also easy not to do.' Is it easy to go for a walk? That question is self-explanatory, as it is so easy to go for a walk but yet we won't or don't do it. We always find excuses for something. Oh if only it was a little bit hotter outside. Oh, if only I didn't have a bad day at work. There is always an excuse for something and you are the only person who can change it. I can't make you do anything or change your mind, it is your decision. I remember doing a year 12 public speaking competition which I happened to win so therefore I remember the topic: 'happiness is a daily choice'. This is 100% accurate and you choose whether you are happy or not, it is simply a state of mind. If you hang around with sad and grumpy people all the time guess what, you are going to be sad and grumpy. Make the decision not to be; everyday is beautiful, we are so privileged to live in the greatest country in the world, yet so many people don't see that or appreciate it and think that they have a horrible life. It is easy to make money, just make it a daily choice and change your mind so that you can change your life!

Now I know that I've already used this before, but I feel that it is important so I'm going to repeat it again. I went to a seminar with Anthony Robbins, and he spoke about when people say to you that money isn't important, it means they are poor. The rich believe and know that money is important; he used the analogy of what is more important, an arm or a leg? We know they are both as important as each other. What if we had the best health in the world but you were homeless and living on the street and eating out of rubbish bins? Is this a very good quality of life? In my opinion not really, so that's why we need both in our lives, money and health!

When people say they can't afford it, or they have a deposit but they don't have any borrowing capacity, or borrowing capacity and no deposit. You need to open your minds, instead of saying I can't afford it, you need to say how can I afford it? For those of you who have read Robert Kiyosaki Rich Dad Poor Dad you will know exactly what I am talking about. What if I said I would give you the money for a deposit, would you then be able to afford it? There are ways to do it you just need to have the right mind set and open your mind up to the fact that there are strategies and ways out there to enable you to reach your goals and become financially free, if this is something that you want to achieve.

Knowing something is one thing and using it and applying it is something completely different. Even if you have all the knowledge in the world, does that make you rich? No, it doesn't, you need to apply this knowledge in order for you to become rich.

How many times do you say "I would do this if I had money" or "I would do that if I could afford it?" People are a lot of talk all the time, then when it comes to 'crunch time' for people to perform and actually do something they rarely do. People want to be right all the time. From an early age you are also recognised and rewarded for being right. A spelling test, 'Good job you got it right,' 'Oh you got 7 out of 10 right congratulations.' This has programmed people from an early age to always want to be right and that being right is good. Therefore, when it comes to investments, people always want to be right and they get scared and don't want to risk any money, or have the fear that they are risking money and place added 'perceived' risk into their heads when there really isn't any there. Why? Because they want to be right. I have a perfect trading example for this. There was this lady who got 9 out of 10 trades right, now this is a very high ratio and you would think that she was making a lot of money, but she wasn't. She was losing lots of money because she had placed a trade for the price to go up, however, if the price were to go down, then she would hold onto them until they went back up again. She wanted to be right. The question remains; do you want to be right or do you want to be rich?

Being rich is not easy; if it were easy everyone would do it. It takes a lot of hard work, you need to have the right mindset and you need a strategy with a plan. People are not amazing at something the first time they try or do something. They work on it and they get better with time and lots of practice. You might not succeed the first time but you need to have persistence. Keep on working towards that goal. Many great millionaires and billionaires have gone broke and yet they have come back bigger and better than ever. If they had of given up the first time then they wouldn't have had the fortunes that they have now.

I repeat again, whether you think you can or your think you can't, you're right.

The strategy for success is:

think → idea → try → do → do again → and again → keep on doing → success

Quiz:

What is your mindset like? Positive or negative?

Do you believe that you can achieve anything that you set your mind to?

Have you done anything to improve yourself?

Do you self-sabotage by saying 'if only'?

If you actually want to finally do something and change your life for the better so you can 'work because you want to and not because you have to,' then register to our website as we are here to help.

http://www.moneysecretsthatwork.com

CHAPTER 25
MARKETING

It could be argued that this is only really important if you are self-employed and thinking about creating your own business. I disagree with that comment as I believe that we all have to be experts at marketing as in reality everything we do is all about marketing. How do you make money? You have to sell something don't you? If people aren't buying anything from you then you will never make any money. So, therefore, everything you do is really a business as you need to make sales. As I mentioned in the introduction chapter, as Robert Kiyosaki points out, you have to always look like your wealthy. You have to sell yourself. People have to like and trust you to buy your product. Even if you are a PAYG employee and are applying for a job, you are still trying to sell yourself to the company so that they will hire you. Then you have to continually do a good job for them so that you don't get fired. Either way everything that you are doing is selling yourself.

The first question people ask is why I should buy from you? If you don't know why people should buy from you then they probably won't.

Lots of people have their own business and I'm sure you would have lots of competitors. If everyone is selling something then you need to do things that are different to your competitors. If you are doing something the same then there is no reason they should buy off you, so you need to have some form of added value. The number one pre requisite of the buying market place is **'perceived added**

value' that's how we choose who to do business with. So if you're a work boot company you need to say 'we made the world's most comfortable work boot guaranteed.' Whatever industry you are in you need to add value under promise and over deliver by exceeding people's expectations. Again if you are applying for a job, what makes you different from anyone else that has the same degree from the same university? You need to give them something that no one else has.

This book is adding value to your life and I aim to educate people and help them to be financially free.

You need to go to a little more effort with people and go that extra yard. If you are a tradesperson, and you are trying to get some money to fund property, if you do a quote for someone and just give them a price on a piece of paper, this is just basic. You need to give them some sort of added value. What if you were to say 'I am happy to give you a quote but I'm also doing jobs in x and y location. Feel free to drop by any time and have a look first hand at the work I am doing.' How much money does this cost you? It doesn't cost you any extra money and yet you are doing something that no one else is doing in the market and this is adding value to the client and building trust. You are much more likely to get the job than just handing them a price on a piece of paper.

Another thing that I find interesting in some companies is that they have very tight budgets for their marketing campaigns. They will find something that is working and say "No, we can only spend x amount of dollars on this particular campaign." If the particular campaign is working, why would you limit how much you could use it? You could spend more money to use it more as it is providing you income. You cannot make any money unless you make sales. If you have to spend money to make sales then that is something that you should do.

Now let's look at marketing in our lives, if you are looking for a new boyfriend or girlfriend you are marketing yourself. If it's a new job you are looking for, you are again marketing yourself. If you have a new idea at work, you need to market the idea to your boss and co-worker. Going for a loan with the bank you are marketing your idea to the bank so they will come on board with you and give you the loan. If you are in sales it is all marketing and problem solving. If you can work out what someone's problem is and then you solve their problem for them you have unlocked the secret to both marketing and sales. In today's world people do not like to be sold to and that is why it is so important to find out what they want and then give them a solution. Once they realise you have solved their problem they will buy from you and come back again and again and again.

SUMMARY

Thank you very much for reading this book. Robert Kiyosaki says at the end of Rich Dad, Poor Dad "all of us were given two great gifts, your mind and your time. It is up to you to do what you please with both."

Hopefully you have learnt something from this book to put you in a position to work because you want to and not because you have to. It is up to you to take action and do something to change your life.

I have put together just a few points that I want to reemphasise for you:

Respect your money

Money is important. What is more important an arm or a leg?

Leverage your money

Income-producing and increasing your residential property portfolio is a proven, long-term, tax effective investment for building wealth

Many of the BRW richest 200 list either made their money in property or store their money in property

You need a mentor, if you don't know something, ask someone who does. You don't need to make the mistakes that everyone else has already made before you. Read biography's and autobiography's of rich people

You need to find out why you want to be rich and work towards that

You must have written goals, you need a plan, no point building a house without any plans, won't end up very good, this is the same in property and investing, you must have a plan and stick to it. Did you know that Apollo 11, the space mission that was first to land on the moon was off course for 97% of the time and the rest of the time it was adjusting, adjusting, adjusting until it finally reached its destination, the moon. So, if it was off course 97% of the time, how did it reach its destination? It did because it had one. What is your destination? Do you in fact have one? If not, where are you going to end up?

If you only learn one thing or take one thing out of this book it should be the jars system as this one strategy alone will get you a long way towards achieving financial freedom enabling you to work because you want to not because you have to.

1. **Financial Freedom Account (FFA)**
   This is a minimum of 10% contribution.
   This account is set up so that you can be in the position where you only work because you want to and not because you have to. This money should only be spent on investments that produce cash flow and/or capital growth

2. **Long Term Savings For Spending Account (LSS)**
   This is a 10% contribution.
   The funds in this account go towards new toys that you want, like a new car, new TV, a new holiday or anything else that you can think of. This account has been great for my dad as he now understands that if he wants to buy something the money has to be in this account first, it has assisted in teaching him to respect money and not just spend it whenever he wants to.

3. **Education Account**
   This is a 10% contribution.
   The funds in this account go towards your constant education and personal development. For example the money you used to purchase this book can come out of the education account. A seminar, university degree or anything to enhance yourself as a person.

4. **Charity Account**
   This is a 5% contribution, although some say it should be 10% and if you want to make it 10% you can take it from the Lon Term Saving for Spending (LSS) account.
   Rich and prosperous people believe in giving back. If you give money away then more money will come back to you. There are people less fortunate than us out there and this is a little something from us that goes a long way for them. The giving also starts now, not only when you are wealthy, as we need to learn how to give in order to be able to receive.

5. **Tax Account**
   This can vary but as a general rule of thumb is a 10% contribution.
   Note: This account is only valid if you are self-employed and should be taken our first before dividing up into the other accounts. You do not need to set this account up if you are a PAYG employee as it will automatically be taken out before you receive your pay cheque.

6. **Play/Fun Account**
   This is a 10% contribution.
   As my mother is a saver and hates to spend money this account has helped her to get used to the idea of spending money and understand that it is ok. The money in this account should be spent every month, or if you want to save up for something a bit more expensive, must be spent at least every 3 months.

7. **Necessity Account**

    This is normally a 55% contribution.

    This account is to pay for your essentials, the standard, shelter and food. If you are living at home, you have lower expenses, less or no rent and you might not spend as much on food. If you have a balance left over this is when you can allocate the balance of the funds towards your financially free account or your long term savings for spending. This is why those accounts have a minimum of 10% contributions.

www.ingramcontent.com/pod-product-compliance
Lightning Source LLC
Chambersburg PA
CBHW071424170526
45165CB00001B/380